LETTERS FROM THE EDGE

A TRAVELOGUE THROUGH THE LOOKING GLASS OF PARALYSIS

Love

J. MICHAEL KANOUFF

J. M. Kanouff

Llumina Press

DEDICATION

More than half my lifetime ago, my father left our family as the result of a car accident. George Kanouff remains a huge figure in my life and I am deeply sorry he's not here today to read these words. I often feel his presence though, in the form of a subtle guidance.

The cover of this book includes an old black and white photo of the two of us looking down from a mountaintop. I combined this ghostly photo with a later image of me, taken just before my injury, in which I appear to be leaping over "The Edge."

I have a sense that there is a greater theme at work in my life and paralysis is part of my life's script. Maybe on that Colorado mountain my father and I made a silent pact to stay by each other's side. I do feel as though he's watching over me from a higher mountain and for his continued love and overseeing protection, I dedicate this book to him.

George Oscar Kanouff
1913-1974

Author's note: As we go to press, the horrific news of Christopher Reeve's passing ripples across the planet. The successful effort he and his family made to live a full and complete life is a story of myth and legend.

If our purpose in life is to be the very best that we can be, then Christopher Reeve and his wife Dana will inspire this and subsequent generations to come. Godspeed Christopher; your work here is done.

Christopher Reeve
1952-2004

ACKNOWLEDGMENTS

After my spinal cord injury, my circle of loved ones wanted to know how I was doing, so I started writing a series of descriptive newsletters chronicling my experience. My friend Mary Lane gave me her ticket to a writer's conference being held on Maui, and it was there that I met the literary agents Michael Larsen and Elizabeth Pomada. Their encouragement made this book a dream that might possibly come true. Then I had a mission.

I was inspired to "report from the front line" on my life in a wheelchair. My circle of newsletter recipients grew into a mailing list of eight hundred people, and their feedback gave me the courage to not only see my challenges, but to continue capturing them in words.

I am deeply grateful to my extended family on this fair island of Maui. Their friendship and selfless volunteering of time and assistance helped me reconstruct my life with a positive perspective. I was privileged to have their company as I metaphorically relearned how to walk and talk.

I am also indebted to my blood family in the Midwest for their constant, loving support and enthusiastic promotion of my writing. They put on multiple fundraisers for my benefit and gave valuable assistance in my having permanent, accessible housing on Maui.

I hold a special appreciation for my longtime friend Saranne Cooke. She remains a daily inspiration for her courage in the face of adversity and her stalwart conviction that life is good under any circumstance.

I owe special thanks to Richard Lafond for compiling my early newsletters into a single manuscript and doing the first edit. He made me feel like an actual book author. Many drafts later, I was running out of steam and was afraid the book might end up as just a good idea until the appearance of my incomparable Beloved. She has elevated my life and this story, and masterfully steered the volume through to the final edit. Her command of the English language, but most of all her love, made this book a reality.

Thank you to all for your love and consideration, given in a myriad of ways. You have enabled me to pen this travelogue about my magical new life.

FOREWORDS

It has now been a full decade that I have known Michael Kanouff. I became aware of his life circumstances with an urgent request from a mutual friend living on Maui, asking if I would be willing to speak at a benefit to help raise the funds to finance a trip to Miami, Florida for an analysis of his spinal cord injuries. That evening, along with Dr. Gerald Jampolsky and Alan Cohen, all voluntarily speaking at a public event on Maui, we had a huge turnout and raised the needed finances to get Michael was on his way.

I was able to meet with Michael in Miami and thus was formulated a close relationship that lives on today. In the ensuing decade I have come to know Michael as an angel of compassion and healing. I encouraged him to write his story and let the people of the world see for themselves the enormous power of the inner spirit in making one's life blissful and complete.

There is much to gain from reading Michael's words describing his ten-year odyssey. No one can uplift others unless they themselves are uplifted. As *A Course in Miracles* reminds us, "Who can bestow upon another what he doesn't have? And who can share what he denies himself?" Michael chose very early on in his experience of paralysis to uplift himself; this has been his journey. And now, with the publication of *Letters from the Edge*, he expands his inner vision based upon his own personal transformation to share with all of us what he refused to deny himself.

You will find no pity or looking back in anger in the pages of this remarkable book. You will find no regrets as you read these powerful messages. You will experience an awareness of the idea that there are no accidents, and that every fall we experience, even those that keep us down for a long, painful period of time, truly provides us with the energy to propel ourselves to higher and higher levels.

The next time you find yourself participating in a "pity party," or feeling overwhelmed by the problems you face, or even feeling anxious or depressed, I urge you to pick up this book and let it remind you of the power of feeling blessed and grateful. Let Michael's words reverberate in your heart and help you to send any self-imposed paralysis out of your life. Let this book remind you that you are not just a body, you are not just a mind, but rather you are the beloved, a reflection of the divine, and that your imagined struggles are nothing more than your curriculum to God. I deeply respect you, Michael. And I send you oceans of love.

Dr. Wayne W. Dyer
Maui, 2004

We all face tragedies and traumas in life that seem insurmountable. I believe that after reading this book, many people will feel their problems are but mosquito bites compared to the challenges that Michael Kanouff has overcome in his life.

This is an awesome book of hope that will put the reader in touch with the Indomitable Spirit that rests in each of us. This book is not just for people who are paralyzed and their loved ones, but for everyone.

Michael writes with an unusual sense of transparency, wisdom and depth and at the same time with a wonderful sense of humor. His determination for life and love reminds me of a sight that most of us have seen and admired: a tree growing and reaching for the sky coming out of what looks like pure granite. The tree's desire for life is so strong that it believes anything is possible. For me, that tree, like Michael, is shouting out for the world to see and to hear: "I am here. I am alive. I am beautiful. I am Spirit and the Essence of Love that will never disappear. I believe and I trust."

Michael demonstrates in his life that he has a sense of resiliency in his being, a rubber bounce that will not allow him to be defeated. He is a master teacher of helping all of us to never give up hope. He is a teacher of perseverance and a teacher of love.

In my heart I know that those of you who read this book will grow to respect Michael, as I and the many people he has touched in his life have, learning lessons in love by just being in his presence.

I love you, Michael. Thanks for the gift you've given us all in writing this book.

Gerald Jampolsky, M.D.
Tiburon, California

If you enjoy this book, contact me for a free subscription to my ongoing, printed newsletters. This book has an ending, but my life experiences will go on and on—and I will write it all down.

J. Michael Kanouff
Kanouff@Maui.net
or visit my web site
fromtheedge.net

CONTENTS

INTRODUCTION

On December 12, 1993, I died. Within one second, I was given a second life, a journey as a quadriplegic. Thus began my travels in a wheelchair, through totally new terrain.

A paralyzing spinal cord injury is one of the ultimate life crises a person can face, but graced by the compassionate support of my family and community, I avoided a terrifying tailspin into depression, loneliness and poverty. Instead, I was able to sail into exciting, uncharted seas of reflection and discovery. I also wrote a few letters along the way.

Taken from a series of newsletters to friends and family over ten years, *Letters* chronicles the incredible, roller coaster, daily life of a quadriplegic. Through my newsletters, friends and family vicariously joined in my travels. A common theme in each letter (and the best way to make sense of this injury) was the growing realization that there is a greater reason for my new life.

In order to maximize the amount of information and diversity within a small book, I maintained the feel of a newsletter in format, with thematic subsections in each chapter. As a photojournalist, I felt compelled to pepper the work with photographs.

This book is meant to be timeless and referential to anyone, so I avoided excessive use of specific dates and names. I also omitted certain unnecessary, gritty details because I wanted to offer a book that would ultimately inspire rather than discourage the reader. Besides, the things that elevate us are what will last, and the grit of life just falls away.

A word to the wheelers: every spinal cord injury is unique. This book narrates how I personally handled my own, but I also learned a lot about how to live in a wheelchair. My sincere hope is that this book will keep some of you from having to reinvent the wheel of decision-making and troubleshooting surrounding various aspects of the new life brought on by paralysis.

A word to the walkers: I invite you to take the time to explore the world of paralysis. Expand your awareness of a country populated with one quarter of a million spinal cord injured people. You will find that curiously enough, when faced with the worst, the best surfaces from people with spinal cord injuries. We can all be inspired by their courage and revelations about the deeper meanings of life.

This is my intimate journal of how ordinary people become Supermen and Wonderwomen through paralyzing spinal cord injuries. In fact, any severe life crisis can galvanize a person into becoming more alive than they had ever imagined before. One can always penetrate the veil of terror and confusion to see the growth of a purposeful new life.

SECTION I

THE EARLY YEARS

*To make an end is to make a beginning; the end is where we start from.
I was photographing a friend's casual wedding at the same beach on which two weeks
later I would be injured. I stood 6'6" tall and loved to take photographs.
I also loved to play Frisbee...*

1

BORN OF THE WATER

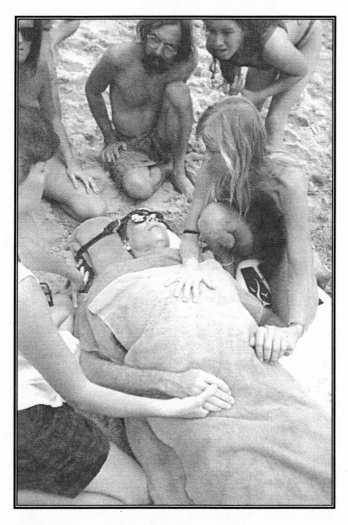

"The vacationing paramedics and two Yale doctors carried me from the water... and with donated belts immobilized my body on a surfboard. Maui must be a magical place, to have had these professionals serendipitously at hand to act as midwives."

I closed my eyes and waited for the tumble of water and sand to subside. The Frisbee had been thrown low, but I made a heroic leap for it anyway, thinking the surf would cushion my fall to the sand; it did not. My head burrowed hard into the sand while the rest of my body somersaulted. My neck snapped. When I couldn't move my arms to push up out of the water, I realized instantly that my life was going to be totally different—if I survived.

Moments before, I'd been sitting on a sand dune, gazing out at the ocean and looking intently within, at the spectrum of my life. I had yet to encounter a beloved in my life. I was at a fork in the road with my career and could go in either direction, both inherently flawed, but also deeply fulfilling. Unfortunately, there was more of the former in both cases, creating an inner angst that was tearing me apart. I was despondent and feeling very alone. I thought a little Frisbee might help…

Face down in the shallow surf, I struggled to conserve my last lungful of air; otherwise, I would burn oxygen and gasp a lungful of salty seawater. My only hope was that someone would see me floating on the water, motionless, and quickly investigate. To panic risked losing my narrow window of survivability, so I concentrated instead on the beautiful dance of sand and water currents beneath me. Simultaneously, I mentally cried out to my friends on the beach, "Come get me! I'm not fooling around, I'm really hurt!"

Burning lungs would soon force open my mouth. Eyes opened wide and stinging from the salt, I screamed inaudibly for help. I was seconds from losing control, seconds from taking the breath that would be my last, when all of a sudden the sand sprouted a forest of hairy legs.

Forty-five seconds had passed before several vacationing paramedics noticed me face down in the water and instantly reacted. My friends, who thought I'd been practicing some exotic water meditation, sprang into action only after the paramedics had already lifted my 6'6", 190-pound body out of the sea. I gasped, "Thank you, oh thank you!" while they yelled, "Support his head!" to my friends. Two other angels present were a husband and wife medical team who taught at Yale. The vacationing paramedics and two Yale doctors carried me from the water, placed me flat on the sandy beach, and with donated belts immobilized my body on a surfboard. Maui must be a magical place, to have had these professionals serendipitously at hand to act as midwives.

As we waited for the ambulance a friend held my hand, and I could hear her softly singing as I began slipping into and out of a euphoric swoon. It was dawning on me that my old life—with all of its pressure, tension and fears—had ended. All of my responsibilities were erased. Of course I knew tremendous challenges were ahead of me, but at the time, I felt like a newborn with no cares.

I also felt the presence of something much larger than myself, a focus of fate moving me along like a strong river current.

"That you, God? Or is it you, Dad? Are you watching this?" I asked haltingly. "If you're there, I have a question: why am I so euphoric in the face of paralysis?"

Trumpets didn't blare, nor was there the booming of a great voice. I simply continued my one-sided conversation, hoping someone was listening. Euphoria, as it turned out, was the best protection I could've had. Maybe this was the way God was talking to me, by giving me the ability to see the promise in an overwhelming situation. Maybe it was pure grace that I immediately latched on to the potential for good and continued to keep a sharpshooter's eye on it.

Sweating under a load of equipment, the ambulance team slogged their way across the sand. I was delicately transferred to their stretcher and firmly strapped down.

"But, but, isn't there supposed to be a helicopter?" I thought. "One of those Coast Guard choppers would do quite nicely."

The beach was secluded by a semicircular wall of lava thirty feet high that had oozed its way down to the ocean two hundred years before. The steep, narrow footpath over the lava wall was too precarious for two paramedics to traverse alone, so nearby surfers were conscripted to hand-over-hand the stretcher to the other side of the volcanic flow. I couldn't bear to watch myself dangling in midair, so I closed my eyes and went back inside. And the paramedics got me safely inside their ambulance.

Although I'd received no direct response from either God or my Dad, I did experience a glowing fire in my chest that left me swooning and serene. If I had to choose between a Godless cause-and-effect universe or a life filled with angels conspiring with a beneficent higher intelligence, then I would choose the latter. There was a reason for my injury. I couldn't see it then, but I was sure there was one.

Bang! With that thought, the ambulance hit a pothole. The rough beach road bounced my head upon the stretcher, painfully jarring me back into my body. My head was on fire. Oddly, the pain I felt wasn't from the paralyzing neck injury, but from the sand embedded in my thick, curly brown hair. It dug into my scalp like tiny shards of glass. That sand would haunt me for the next three days. My head was put in traction, and no one wanted to wash my hair for fear of further damaging my spine.

I would have many conversations with God in the coming years, and a few times He even talked back. His voice was heard in lessons learned through painful experiences, which forced my eyes to see and my ears to hear, and in heart-opening realizations of the inherent divinity of human nature.

ER

Word of my injury had spread like wildfire across the island. Over thirty friends raced to the ER, overflowing the waiting room. Seated side-by-side they waited for news, some dressed in their Sunday best, others fresh from the beach in their swimming suits.

The initial injury trauma didn't cause the major damage; rather, subsequent swelling of the spinal cord in the vertebral column had choked off the vital blood supply to delicate nerve fibers. To prevent further damage, the emergency room staff at Maui Memorial Hospital continued to administer the anti-inflammatory IV drug started in the ambulance.

Once the ER staff had stabilized me, they then administered tranquilizers and pain medications—none of which helped the searing pain in my scalp from the embedded sand. With a traction neck brace installed, I was loaded into another ambulance and taken to the airport. Next stop: Queen's hospital trauma center, three islands away in Honolulu.

I was suddenly alone in the hold of an old twin engine plane. My stretcher was strapped atop three rows of threadbare passenger seats. The forty-five minute, low altitude transport further vibrated the dagger-like sand into my skull. Never had I experienced such pain! My only refuge was my breath. It was during those moments that I understood the value of Lamaze breathing for pain control. Deep, connected breaths kept me from losing it.

Intensive Care Conversations

Three ambulances, one airplane and numerous gurneys transported me around and from Maui until I finally landed in the Queen's hospital intensive care unit. Left unattended for a few moments during my intake, I reviewed what had just happened.

The intense shock from the injury maintained my odd sense of euphoria. My known world had ceased to exist. Every petty fear and concern became totally irrelevant, my thinking had an unusual clarity and I sensed I was not alone. All of this was immensely comforting, as I remembered an ancient Chinese proverb that says, "The first step of a thousand mile journey determines your destination."

I pondered, "If I am beginning a new life, I must see all of the good that can come out of this injury right from the start in order to protect my sanity. This could be the fast track to something great in my life. And if so, is this really an event to be mourned, or an initiation into some elite priesthood?"

The cacophony of the modern intensive care room around me faded into the background. My thoughts began to resonate as if I were in a large, silent hall. Realization of the gravity of the situation then pushed all thoughts from my mind. From the resulting stillness, a soothing reassurance emerged that wasn't heard, just understood. "You are not going to die. This nightmare will eventually pass."

"Good," I thought to myself. "That's the bottom line. Knowing that will keep me back from the edge of hysteria."

"Will I walk again?" I whispered.

No answer.

"What do I do now?" I asked silently.

A certainty came from deep within that I shouldn't look too far ahead or the enormity of the situation would overwhelm me. I was to stay in the present and live each moment fully, put blinders on my eyes and trust that I would be supported. Decisions and actions that would come from being totally in the present would be the conscious footsteps needed for this journey. Everything would unfold gracefully.

"Will I be strong enough?" I wondered.

Despite facing one of the most trying health crises a person can experience, I felt capable and strong. Obviously there would be intense challenges ahead, but for the first time in my life, I had permission to be weak and vulnerable. Paradoxically, this opened up the entire spectrum of living to me as never before. I felt reduced to nothing, and thus could become anything.

"Will I be happy?" I mused.

Another wave of euphoria washed through me. As it receded, I was left wet with the knowledge that my life's purpose was on track, a bizarre feeling to experience when strapped tightly to a table with fluid dripping into and electrodes draping off of my body. But there it was: a sure knowledge that I was doing what I was meant to do. This knowing was as deep and true as the knowledge a woman holds that she is pregnant.

Any doubt about my life's purpose vaporized without a trace. The most important time in my life had begun. I couldn't see ahead around the bend on my new road of life, but I knew where I'd been before.

PAST LIFE

If you want to get physically away from civilization, Hawaii is the place to go. Centered thousands of miles from the nearest landfall, in the middle of the Pacific Ocean, is a string of tiny islands including Maui, which is 30 miles long and 10 wide. How the early Polynesian navigators found this string of sultry pearls in the middle of all this water is beyond me. I just got on an airplane in San Francisco in 1985.

I knew Hawaii used dollar bills, zip and area codes like the rest of America, but to me she was a third world country—an adventure. My first taste of Hawaiian life was the island of Maui. She had a wonderful old airport without passenger tubes snaking to each plane. I exited onto the top of an old staircase leading to the tarmac. The air was soft, humid, and thick with the scent of exotic flowers. I felt instantly and sweetly intoxicated, and wobbled down the steps with my camera bag.

I'd come on a rare vacation and halfway through my stay decided paradise was to be my next home. I later met many others who'd made similar snap decisions about moving to Hawaii. They'd arrived as tourists from all over the world and immediately fell in love with her nurturing weather, culture and environment. Then they all fell in love with each other as a community. Hawaii felt like the right place and they just stayed. The want ads were filled with return air tickets for sale.

Moving to Hawaii from California was a leap into the unknown. Like many other recent arrivals, I was searching. The beautiful climate, azure blue waters and wild, lush tropical forests were the obvious attractions. Or maybe it was the reverberating resonance of the native Hawaiian people that made these islands sacred and a lure to the sensitive soul. I knew Hawaii would be my next base of operations.

As a freelance photographer, I planned to live on Maui and frequently fly back to "America" to service my clients. At the end of my vacation, I was offered a place to stay. I was to share a house with some kindred spirits. Like members of a tribe, they would become the foundation of an extended family that would play a large role in helping me to survive my injury.

My home was a large, multiple-bedroom beach house. I was single and shared the house with a roommate and a seminar production company. Between working on the computer and taking photographs, I would often walk out the door and leap into the ocean, just thirty feet away. Life in paradise was good!

ON THE TRAIL OF TEARS

All my life I've been able to express my emotions through crying, not in huge volumes, but I could always tear at a good movie or a poignant example of the human spirit shining through adversity. After my injury, which put me in direct contact with my emotional body, I could cry at the drop of a hat.

I believe we humans protect ourselves from emotional trauma by muscle armoring, the tightening of our muscles in preparation for "fight or flight." Every painful experience not expressed and cleared gets stored in our bodies. Chiropractors, Rolfers and deep tissue massage therapists all stay very busy because of the work they do releasing the muscle armor protecting our emotional bodies. Like a cage, this armoring holds in our emotions and deadens us to the joys of life.

Notice how young children will laugh, clap, and jump with glee while listening to a *Sesame Street* song. This explosion of life sharply contrasts to the young adult stiffly jerking around on a dance floor, "trying to loosen up." I make this point because of a profound gift I received from my injury—I lost most of my body armoring! I attributed my amplified ability to cry, laugh, feel another's pain and absorb the beauty of a setting sun to the complete relaxation of most of my body's muscles.

I could cry openly and readily; not mourning my condition, but celebrating the love I felt from all my friends. Every visiting friend at the hospital got a chance to cry with me. Every time someone reached out to me in the form of a telephone call, a card in the mail, flowers sent to my room or a visit in person, I thanked them with heartfelt tears. I felt no shame connected to my crying, just a deep release of age old tension and a healing balm of love.

BACK ON THE LANDING PAD

"What is your social security number Mr. ahh... Canoe-uff?"

My eyes slowly opened. Towering over me with her head on the ceiling was a clipboard woman wearing a generic, pastel-colored uniform. It was the tenth time I'd rattled off my personal identity number. After more redundant questions, she finally allowed my waiting friends to enter.

My room in intensive care was a bit of a madhouse those first few hours. My feeling was that I had died and didn't know it, and everyone was filing by to pay their respects. While my old self had indeed been left behind, I remained among the living. Instead of my next of kin getting cards and telephone calls expressing gratitude for me, I got to experience everyone's gratitude firsthand.

People flowed in and circled my bed. The room would fill up between the blinking of my eyes. Some were asked to leave and visit in shifts. My heart exploded with affection for these dear friends who had dropped everything and hopped on the next plane to Oahu from Maui.

As they approached my bed, their expressions revealed shock and concern. Most wanted to hear rehashings of the injury. Some had frozen smiles, others blank looks of disbelief; many had watery eyes that melted the distance between us. But only a few of my closest friends had the courage to start the conversation that seemed it would never end. They asked, "What do we do next?"

THE NEVER ENDING STORY

Hospitals, insurance companies, Social Security, state health departments, Medicaid, nursing agencies, Medicare and the Department of Housing and Urban Development—once obscure bureaucracies to me—were suddenly an intimate part of my new world.

My dear friends took on the bureaucratic dragons and left me to face my own fire-breathing fears. The first agenda item was to contact my health insurance company. My friends were told that my policy didn't include catastrophic coverage and would be depleted in ten days' time.

My only option was to apply for Medicaid, health insurance for the poor. One friend jumped into my papers and proved I was (un)worthy; I made it under the financial wire of need by fifty-seven cents! My healthcare bills would be paid, thanks to the simplicity of my bachelor lifestyle. If I had owned a house, property, stocks, retirement fund—anything besides a car and $2,000 worth of possessions—it all would've been liquidated immediately to cover medical costs. It's only after you've hit rock bottom that Medicaid will come to your rescue.

I became a believer that everyone should have at least catastrophic health coverage. With a high deductible, the yearly cost is very reasonable and if tragedy strikes, there are more choices for healthcare. Medicaid is a safety net only for the desperately poor. Any assets one has—a house, property, savings, investments—have to be liquidated to pay for medical bills before Medicaid even becomes possible. Medical expenses can quickly consume a family's life savings or college funds, an added insult to injury that shouldn't occur.

CEILINGS: BOY, DO I KNOW CEILINGS

I had been lying exclusively on my back since the beachside injury, so I really got to study the fine art of ceilings—first in the ambulance, moving on to the Maui ER, then in the plane to Honolulu, back in another ambulance, and ending finally in the intensive care unit. From the molded plastic, easy-to-clean ambulance roofs to the ever present drop ceiling panels, our horizontal protectors became my friends.

Quite often I was rolled around the hospital on gurneys, to lie in wait for a testing room to open up. The hospital aide would disappear and I was left in the hallway without someone with whom to make idle chatter. So I continued my study of ceilings. If they were made of square, acoustical tiles, like the ones in high school with hundreds of little holes, I would try to count the holes. Then I would pretend they were stars and squint to see constellations of bunny rabbits or sharks. I was always critiquing each ceiling for its workmanship and could tell the age of the hospital wings by the degree of yellowing on the ceiling tiles.

From early on I kept thinking, "This is where more art should be hung. Vertical people have art on their walls. It would be nice if horizontal people had something of aesthetic value to look at in their rooms and hallways. How about a contiguous mural on the ceiling? The hospital should at least have something in the children's wing."

During my hospital stay, I was always lying on my back. I looked up to see only the ceilings of my room, the hallway, or the smallest confines of an x-ray room. In my peripheral vision, I could only see the stalwart walls supporting the ceiling.

I was always in a box.

One day I was on a gurney being transferred to another box, watching the ceiling go by overhead. Peripherally, I saw sunlight streaming through the wide doors of a hospital side entrance. I asked the orderly if we could pop outside for just a moment. He agreed, so we took a right-hand turn and glided through the electronic doors.

We only needed to go a few feet from the building to get an unobstructed view of just the sky. The colors overwhelmed me. The richest blue of tropical sky nearly blinded me at first. Dappled, fast moving clouds were ceiling tiles in motion; ever changing, performing only for me. Incredibly green coconut palm trees held up the heavens, even as they swayed in the wind. My eyes relaxed as they focused on infinity.

The experience only lasted a few minutes, because the orderly got nervous that we'd gone AWOL. We returned to the fluorescent-lit hallways and rooms. My old friends the white ceiling tiles were waiting for me, but I had a vivid and colorful memory to project upon them.

DEM BONES

"This will sting a little bit," the surgeon whispered as he pricked my temple with the needle. The anesthetic was to dull the bite of the traction harness grip pinching both sides of my head. These pincers pressed through the skin until they had a purchase on my skull. My immobilized head was then connected by rope to a weight hanging off the top of my bed.

The surgeon wanted the swelling in my spinal cord to go down before repairing my fractured vertebrae. I had to wait five days with my head constantly clamped to the 40-pound traction weight, while bags of anti-inflammatory liquid dripped into my bloodstream. Unable to turn my head, I looked for repeating patterns in the ceiling tiles, a mind game I remembered playing in grade school.

With no outside window view to judge whether it was day or night, coupled with broken sleep patterns, the five-day wait to surgery seemed like an eternity. Only my diaphragm was breathing for me and I had an inordinate fear that if I fell asleep, I would stop breathing. After sleeping a few minutes, I would explode awake, gasping for air. I was quite crazed after five days of sleeping on a roller coaster.

Fortunately, I was rarely alone. A friend was almost always nearby to hold my hand. Even when I awoke from a tortured sleep, someone was usually next to my bed, asleep in the reclining chair.

THE CONVERSATION CONTINUES

The night before surgery, as the intensive care machines beeped and whirred, my mind drifted restlessly back to the questions, "Will the surgery be successful? Will I be left in pain? What if something goes drastically wrong?"

I was told these surgeries were commonplace and that I had nothing to fear. But it sure would've been easier to relax into the experience of going under the knife if God had spoken out loud to me, in person.

"Will I be all right?" I demanded out loud at around midnight, before the dawn surgery.

My roommate stirred, but again, no words from above. A quiet peacefulness washed over me instead.

One thought filled my mind: "Surrender to this unstoppable momentum in your life by trusting that you'll be supported through this transition."

Or, as my father would often say, "Don't worry. Things will always work out." One of the hardest things for me to do was to completely let go of control over a situation and just plain trust. At that moment of my life it was time for complete surrender to the professionals. What choice did I have anyway? I decided that I would just not worry, stay alive to each moment and try to get some sleep.

A deep serenity stayed with me as I lightly slept through to dawn.

OPERATION ADAM'S APPLE

Nurses bustled about preparing me for surgery, and I watched each procedure with fascination. Seconds before being wheeled out of the room, I remembered my camera. "When there is a break in the action, would you take a couple of photographs?" I asked one of the nurses. She smiled and slipped the camera under her surgical gown. My gathered friends, who knew me as a rabid photojournalist, merely groaned.

I reasoned that if my new life had a higher purpose, then it was worth documenting photographically. Little did I know then that my writing, rather than my photography, would ultimately paint the most vivid pictures of my experience.

I was wheeled into the surgical suite, where an injection washed my consciousness away. The doctors had described my injury as a "teardrop burst" fracture at the fifth vertebra. Bone was harvested from my hip for later use, to fuse vertebrae four, five and six. The neurosurgeon then incised a two-inch opening to the right of my Adam's apple, cutting along a neck wrinkle to mask the scar. He moved the throat aside to gain access to the damaged cervical bone and fitted the harvested hipbone over the injury site. A titanium plate was then screwed over all three vertebrae, holding the pieces of hipbone in place and giving them support until they fused to the vertebrae, a six-month process. Finally, he stitched up the incision, and pouf! My life was saved. This was all magic to me. What an amazing world.

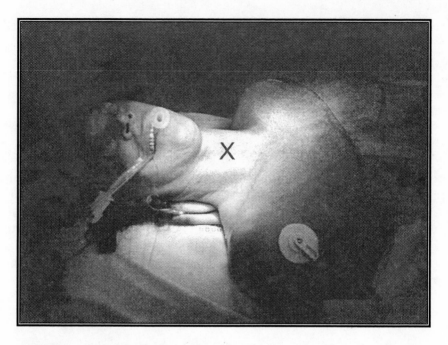

X marks the spot! This surgery was quite remarkable. To hide the scar, the surgeon cut along a wrinkle on my neck. I was deeply impressed with the whole procedure and quite glad I remained unconscious throughout.

If I'd had my injury a few years earlier, I would've been forced to live with a "halo" after surgery, a hellish contraption truly born out of a Middle Ages torture chamber. A ring of metal is screwed into the skull at various points all around the head. Metal braces emerge from padded shoulders to buttress the ring. The purpose is to support the head and prevent movement of the fusing bones—for six long months!

Thank goodness for that titanium plate! The support it gave my healing bones saved me from wearing a halo. I did wear a removable cervical collar for two weeks, just in case someone dropped me. I took it off for my first shower. The evil sand daggers were out of my hair!

OPEN AROUND THE CLOCK

The Queen's hospital critical care facility had a very sane policy of allowing me to receive visitors around the clock. I was very needy those first two weeks, and the nursing staff couldn't always be by my side. So the call was put out and in came the friends, three shifts a day around the clock.

I called for assistance often. Not being able to move was a new thing for me, and I needed help eating, brushing my teeth, scratching my nose and adjusting my television. I had to have letters written, phone calls made, decisions decided and my hand held.

There was such a flow of people from Maui that I shipped my car over to Honolulu for them to drive to and from the airport. Folks had completely stopped their normal lives to camp out on a La-Z-Boy in another city, performing service under stressful circumstances. These volunteers formed a bond that linked them on a deep level. From the stories I heard, many became fast friends because of their shared experience. I believe their lives grew richer from those displays of compassion, because it just feels good to give.

My mother and third eldest sister had flown in from the Midwest in time for my surgery. It was terrific having blood family at the hospital. There was nothing like holding the hands of my Mom and sister when things were grim. They helped make some of the hardest decisions, including what kind of surgery to have and where to go for the two and a half months of rehabilitation. The first decision, about the surgery, was correct. The second, choosing the Honolulu rehab hospital, was, well… a challenging learning experience I could've done without. But I knew how to make it a positive life lesson.

KANSAS CITY BLUES

Hand in hand with my physical therapy was personal therapy. Because the injury had released all physical responsibilities, my mind was able to cross onto the fast track towards a deeper self-reflection. The sheer enormity of the injury brushed aside all the little things that I had thought were important in my life, leaving me with a powerful, long forgotten memory.

The time was the winter of 1974 and I was a student at the Kansas City Art Institute. One blustery night, alone and shivering in my studio apartment, I wrapped in a sleeping bag to ward off the cold (remember the energy crisis?). I was despondent and forlorn, but at the depths of these feelings an inspiration broke through. I promised myself, my God and family that I would do whatever was needed to make it in this lifetime—to fulfill the goal of knowing my soul's reason for existence. I remember immediately wishing I hadn't said that, because I knew the process wasn't going to be easy, but it was too late. I couldn't take it back!

So in conjunction with physical therapy, I decided to work through my core life issues. Every aspect of who I thought I was came up for review, like a spring cleaning of the soul. Resistance seemed futile; my forced sabbatical from most activities of normal life eliminated all smokescreens to this kind of introspection.

I'd been given a life of minimal responsibilities—no children or spouse, no mortgage or debt payments and no professional expectations. I didn't even have a pet! I consciously asked for this cosmic set-up, so I knew I had better take full advantage of this potent opportunity.

A medical crisis can be a powerful tool for spiritual evolution. This perspective has been the key to my recovery and has also changed my view of humanity's ills. Rather than seeing wars, social injustice, environmental suicide and sexual dysfunction as proof that we're all doomed, I perceive these illnesses as part of the process of Life unfolding, a new Life struggling through the birth canal.

There is a need in us to associate with others who share this vision of the Phoenix in all of us, raising our wings from the fires of transformation. We can help keep each other from falling into pits of mediocrity and depression by holding the vision of a higher process at work. My loved ones constantly whispered in my ear that there was a transforming reason for my injury, to which I nodded in agreement, smiling.

I really went for that Frisbee and although I didn't wish to be paralyzed, once I was in the fast lane, I decided to make the most of this incredible momentum of life.

2

IN THE NURSERY

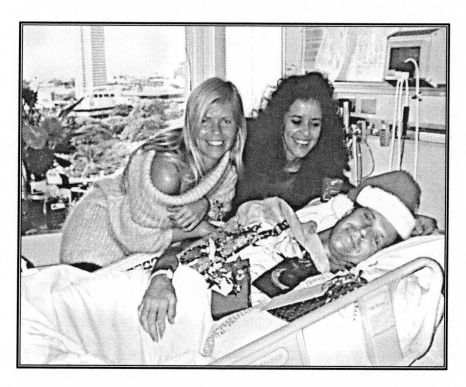

*"Being near my extended family was the best therapy of all... every day I had
a different visiting friend to hold my hand and lift my spirits."*

C hristmas decorations in a hospital feel contrived. Nothing can
overshadow the overwhelming air of a medical bureaucracy
that unfeelingly moves patients along like objects on a
conveyor belt. The daily visits from friends, however, helped push back
the rehab hospital's dark, mechanistic pall. Their presence told me I
was special, while the medical bureaucrats ran the broken record of
"You are a quad. Be quiet and learn to love your wheelchair." Granted,
I was not in a rehab facility for the heavily insured, where patients
could afford to be treated as individuals.

I had chosen to "get on my feet" close to home, at the Rehab Hospital of the xxxxxxx in Honolulu, a run-down place that in 1993 looked like it belonged in a third world country. The nurses, therapists and doctors were overworked and underpaid. Although a couple of bright stars illuminated that dark complex, I found most of the staff to be patriarchal and demeaning. I'd flown into the cuckoo's nest of "Big Nurses." The physical therapists flapped the largest wings.

When I was finally released two and a half months later, I felt more emotionally scarred by my rehab experience than by breaking my neck. In fact, my original intention in chronicling my experiences was to detail the daily traumas of life at the rehab hospital. But I soon changed my mind. The petty personnel and amateurish therapy quickly crumbled into the past; that time was history. Besides, I didn't want to spit bile for spite. As it turned out, my first weeks in a wheelchair were also magical, challenging and inspiring, which is what I choose to remember.

But I do have to give one account...

URRGE AHAA GLUSH MAIAH URRGHS

Initially, the rehab hospital didn't even want me. Typically, only blood family members took on the responsibility of caring for the spinal cord injured in their homes. The staff suggested I go back to Omaha, Nebraska to live with my relatives. They had never heard of friends becoming caregivers. Once released from rehab, they didn't want me to be abandoned and left without care. In addition, if my care faltered, the state would be forced to take me into one of their expensive nursing homes. So I rallied the troops and proved I had a huge extended family network and support system. I was in. I would eventually go back home to Maui. But first I had to survive the rehab hospital.

Immediately after my injury, I spent two weeks in Queen's hospital, a modern critical care facility, where I was treated with kid gloves. After surgery I was transferred off to the rehab hospital, where therapists welcomed me with boxing gloves.

To contrast the facilities, at the first hospital, six people would transfer me prone from bed to a flat-lying wheelchair. Then the chair back was slowly raised, inch by inch, to a vertical position, to ensure that the blood in my head didn't go flooding down into my legs.

Normally, people get out of bed by using their leg muscles, which act as a second heart. Contraction of the muscles constricts and pumps the blood supply to the upper reaches of the body. Post-injury, the muscles in my lower body remained flaccid and blood would pool down to my legs and ankles. If I sat up too quickly in a wheelchair, blood would drain from my head and I would pass out, forced to take an unscheduled nap.

At the second facility, transfers were not as graceful. Within my first hour at the rehab hospital, I was flung over an orderly's back like a sack of potatoes, hung upside down looking at his behind, and dropped into a wheelchair. I knew immediately something was wrong, but couldn't say anything! I could hold words in my mind, but had no idea how to get them out. Then everything in sight melted to white.

A visiting volunteer saw the wild, frightened expression in my eyes and yelled, "Something's wrong! Get him down!"

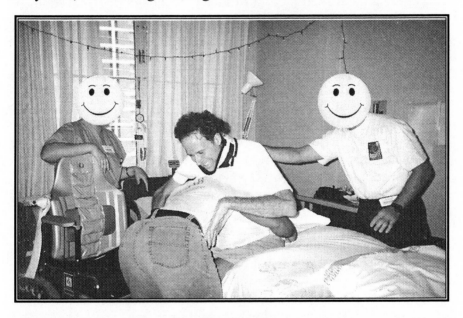

Kids, don't try this at home—you might lose your nouns! With his shoulder pressed into my stomach, this orderly hoisted me upside down into the air and plopped me into the wheelchair. It was this kind of transfer that gave me a minor stroke, which afflicted my speech center, on my first day at the rehab hospital.
(Faces hidden to protect the... innocent.)

Nurses poured into my room, threw the back of the chair down to the floor and furiously pressed my stomach, pumping blood to my ashen head. My vision returned, but I couldn't speak; I'd had a stroke. On top of my spinal injury, I *now* had to communicate with head nods and child-like grunts! Not surprisingly, I was more afraid of not being able to speak than the prospect of living in a wheelchair.

Back I went to the first hospital for CAT scans and neurological evaluation. The doctors said the damage was minor and my speech would return, but to return to near normal would take months, and some damage would always remain. The place where my brain stores nouns was afflicted, so I had a hard time finding them. "Hand me the plate" became "Hand me that white, round thing." For the first time in my life, I had to concentrate on every syllable and every word. This was my darkest period, but eventually the sun came out and six months of intense concentration later, I could once again order take-out pizza.

NON-WHITE CHRISTMAS

The stroke checked me out of the rehab hospital. Because of the paperwork, I couldn't return until after the Christmas season—ten days later. I was livid. I liked the critical care facility at Queen's hospital, but it was too darn cold. Normally, body temperature is regulated by shivering and sweating. With some of my circuits down, my body's thermostat wasn't receiving certain commands from the brain that help to regulate body temperature. I felt like a lizard, subject to fluctuations in exterior temperature. And I had to freeze through Christmas and New Year (Thank goodness no one could understand my ravings!).

Volunteers transferred my room accessories back to Queen's, from where they had just been removed hours before. Now let me tell you about my room, my little lifeboat in the turbulent seas of a new life. Bright cards and posters festooned the walls and ceiling. Little colored Christmas lights brightened my nights and lifted my spirits. An illegal video tape player was connected to the television and a phone machine was plugged into the wall. Colorful wall hangings and dozens of potted plants put the finishing touches on a room for a renegade patient. All of this (and more) had to be shuttled back and forth between the hospitals.

Christmas and New Year came and went. I watched Chinese New Year fireworks through my tiny slit of a window. These were holidays like I had never celebrated before.

My paperwork for re-admittance finally cleared and I was ready to try again at the rehab hospital. Despite the lack of professionalism and compassion, I still believed my choice of a rehab center close to my Maui home was the correct one. Being near my extended family was the best therapy of all. A rotating schedule of volunteers meant that every day I had a different visiting friend to hold my hand and lift my spirits. I felt connected to a loving family that wasn't going to let me go through this dark time alone.

It did get very dark spending three months at Hawaii's only rehab hospital for stroke victims and the newly paralyzed. My main critique of my physical therapists, occupational therapists and one doctor was that they didn't work with me as a team. They all performed their daily therapies in a distant, mechanical fashion, and check-marked a box on a form that I had to sign. I heartily suggest to anyone recently paralyzed, if you have a choice, go to a facility that is proud of its teamwork and incorporates you fully into the therapeutic experience.

A HISTORY LESSON

Although quadriplegic from my injury, I understood my life to be blessed in many ways. Most people would think this was crazy, but consider the following: it has only been in the past century that people have even been able to survive spinal cord injury. Before that, paralysis was survivable only long enough to say goodbye to loved ones. The body's communication links would go down and without a fully functioning nervous system, when the bladder filled it would rupture into the body cavity, because nothing would signal the sphincter muscle to release the urine. Toxicity and a high fever would ensue, quickly taking a life.

Along came a fellow named Foley, who in 1918 invented the rubber catheter, a little snake that pushes past the sphincter and into the bladder, safely draining urine away. But even so, people with paralysis continued to die from severe bladder infections until the development of antibiotics after World War II. Since then, multiple technological advancements have continued to make life with paralysis survivable and more comfortable. So for all the thousands of generations of people on this planet, I became one of an elite few, a tiny percentage, to survive a spinal cord injury thanks to catheters and antibiotics. I think I'm fortunate.

Breathing can also be affected by injury to the spinal cord. In my case, because the spinal column was fractured between the fifth and sixth vertebrae, my lung-to-brain connection was compromised, leaving me unable to swell my lungs with air. I'm not just a fond memory in peoples' minds because the body is so smart; it has backup systems. Although my direct lung connection was damaged, the spinal cord nerves connected to my diaphragm were above the injury site and remained intact. Thus I could still breathe on my own, because my diaphragm could suck air in and through my lungs.

I feel lucky; break the connection above the fifth cervical and one needs that wonderful invention called a respirator, an artificial breather of one's breath. Have you noticed the way Christopher Reeve speaks in a metered, cyclical rhythm? His respirator paces him. Air is pumped into the lungs through an opening cut into the throat and exiting air passes over the vocal cords, allowing him to speak.

Progress has moved so fast in spinal cord research that his high level of injury wasn't even survivable in the 1980s. In fact, within the first few years of the 21st century, Christopher Reeve received one of the first artificial stimulators for the diaphragm. Similar to a pacemaker for the heart, an embedded device electrically stimulates his diaphragm to contract, thus, when it's activated, freeing him from the respirator. By allowing him to breathe through his mouth and nose, this wonderful device also restores his senses of taste and smell.

These and other advancements have taken us way beyond mere survival to pursuing the physical Holy Grail—walking. What an amazing slice of time on the planet. When I expand my focus beyond the daily grind, I can see that this is indeed a wonderful time to be alive.

If we, as a planet, can go through our own process of dying to the old paradigms and being born again into higher levels of truth, what a wonderful world it would be for our grandchildren. Let's not forget about them.

FOUNTAIN OF YOUTH

I often thought of my new life as a rebirth and a learning process. Dormant memories of a previous time shimmered up to the surface of my awareness like old friends at a class reunion. Once, in the rehab hospital, while struggling to control a toothbrush strapped to my hand, connected to an arm with only half the muscles responding, I flashed back thirty-seven years to a similar struggle. The blue tile countertop was at eye level, forcing me to stand on my tiptoes and stretch to wet my toothbrush. My brushing movements were jerky and labored. This was completely new for my three-year-old body.

This struggle to train young muscles was matched only by the effort to learn to tie my shoes, but this was what being a kid was all about—learning new things. As children, we were all faced with training our bodies to do completely new and unique actions. Potty training, tooth brushing, bike riding, handwriting, shoe tying, tree climbing, dishwashing and hiding from angry sisters were all instances where we had to be aware of and discipline our thinking in order to master our muscles. These learning curves were short when we were young, because we were mentally and physically pliable.

At forty years of age, I was returned to learning how to brush my teeth! Awkward jabs at the rear molars contorted my face. My determination this time came not from my mother hovering over me, nor from the fact that I had to learn this for the survival of my teeth, but from a "youthing" effect.

I found my mental attitude freshened and rejuvenated after going through the struggle of learning a new physical ability. Rapid learning was a hallmark of our early years and when new neural pathways to our bodies' muscles were formed, consciousness expanded. For the most part, however, this burst of learning stopped after the required high school gym class or college typing course. Yet continuing the process of learning new physical skills keeps the psyche loose and malleable at any age.

If we're smart, we will all retain the student aspect of our personalities. Regardless of age, if you go after something totally new, your effort will force you to become more open and childlike—the "youthing" effect. Laid-off executives who start their own home businesses may struggle to learn how to type and navigate a computer, but they'll end their days a bit brighter and feel more aware of the colors of life because of their efforts. In this same way, we can all value our days measured by new successes, rather than being haunted by how far we have seemingly fallen in previous failure.

RITUALS

Immediately following my injury, I was reminded of the greatest gift of all, loving friends and family. For three weeks after my injury, I had three shifts of visitors per day. I dreaded those first nights in the hospital. Listless sleep filled with phantom images tortured me. Sleep deprivation was exacerbated if my lungs were congested, because lung-clearing coughs would awaken me. When more air pressure was needed for coughing and clearing my lungs than my diaphragm could produce, a night-shift friend would stumble over from the chair where they'd been sleeping to perform a modified Heimlich maneuver. On some nights, this ritual had to be performed every thirty minutes.

Another hospital survival ritual was to be catheterized every four hours, around the clock (tick tock!). My kidneys still worked and my bladder still filled, but the sphincter remained tightly locked. Since a ruptured bladder would've been death, every four hours I had a rubber catheter snaked up my you know what to drain my bladder. Ooouuch!

This went on six times a day, seven days a week. Amazingly, I became so used to it that I could almost sleep through the 2 a.m. "cathing," but I could never stay asleep through the 2:30 a.m. "turning."

Remember the television reports showing studies on sleep? Through a black-and-white camera mounted on the ceiling, a person in bed was shown tossing and turning throughout the night. The body's innate intelligence detects when it's been in one position too long. The tissues, being starved of blood, send the message "You gotta turn over now."

"Wake up!" said the nurse as she flipped on the light. "Time to turn over."

It was 2:30 in the morning and I had just gotten back to deep sleep following the 1 a.m. turning and the 2 a.m. cathing. She performed the intricate ritual of maneuvering my lanky frame to its other side and stuffing pillows around me to hold the position. I murmured "Thank you" and drifted back to sleep. Lights out until the 4 a.m. turning, a mere ninety minutes away.

Another "every thirty minutes" rehab ritual was doing "pressure relief" in the wheelchair. Just like the ritual bed turning, I had to shift my weight in the hard, crummy rehab chair every half hour to prevent getting pressure sores on my buttocks. Shifting my weight forward allowed blood flow to rush back into the tiny capillaries of my *gluteus maximus*. The physical therapist had put the fear of God into me by showing photos of skin breakdown on other patients. Dying skin and muscle can ulcerate to the bone and it could take months of bed rest and possibly even surgery to heal this depth of wound. Needless to say, I watched the clock—religiously. Every thirty minutes I got to take a "time out" from whatever I was doing to perform a mandatory kissing of the knees.

My manual wheelchair had a chest strap that held me upright. I would release its velcro and loop my wrists through two auxiliary side straps. With wheels locked, I would say goodbye to the vertical world and fall forward, kissing my knees, and from one to three minutes study the scratches on the tile floors. When the scratches started to wriggle like snakes, I knew I was close to passing out. Time to pull myself up, struggle out of the wrist straps and secure the chest strap. Every thirty minutes of nine hours a day for six months, I bowed at the "Altar of the Knees." The clock ruled my life (tick tock!).

SYMBIOSIS

(A relationship of mutual benefit or dependence)

People often asked me the big question after my injury: for all that I was going through, had I ever considered suicide? I admit the thought was occasionally entertained during those early days, but only at my darkest moments. Many reasons held me back, two of which were that I couldn't figure out how to do it by myself and it wouldn't have been fair to my family and friends, who were working so hard to keep me going. And then came another...

A friend confided in me that he was going through hell and had been a moment away from ending it all, foot on the gas pedal, cliff splayed out before him. I came up in his review of life. He felt my predicament to be worse than his and if I could bear mine, he could bear his. Well, the car lived to drive another day and living in my chair became easier, knowing that he still walked because I still couldn't.

Some people admired my spirit and frame of mind, yet I considered the support of friends and family crucial to my survival. I in turn inspired them—a life affirming symbiosis. Besides, I couldn't kill myself because my injury had cooked my soul and burned off vast amounts of unnecessary slag. I couldn't walk but I sure could see far better than before, hear through the din of everyday life and feel deeply rooted emotions of being alive like I never had before the injury. I was in the ultimate personal growth workshop that never ends. I attended every day's session and always had a chair.

GET THE POINT?

While at the rehab hospital I was inundated with cards, letters, phone calls and suggestions for alternative therapies. I tried as many as possible, since I could never tell from which direction the universe would weave its magic. Alternative therapists streamed through my room and did their best to revitalize me. The hospital wasn't too keen on other practitioners working on me under their roof, so we went underground. It was like *Mission Impossible*.

My Honolulu volunteer coordinator was the lookout. Just after dinner and before the 8 p.m. turning, she would hang a "Do Not Disturb" sign on the door and sit in a chair to block the entry. The privacy curtain around the bed was pulled for further protection. Like clockwork, the acupuncturist would exit the stairwell near my room (thus avoiding the nurses' station by the elevator) and give the secret knock at the door. Sliding in, he would be followed a few minutes later by the reflexologist or chiropractor, naturopath, etc. We would all giggle at the success of our intrigue. I was sorry we had to be covert, but knew that the traditional medical model didn't have all the answers.

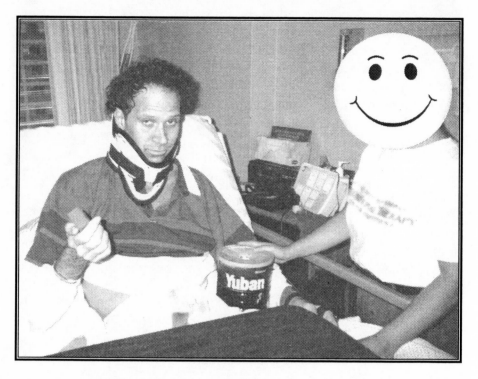

Hmmm... stuffing cubes of foam into a coffee can with a hole in the top—high tech physical therapy? I came to understand that not all rehab hospitals are created equal and that I would have to take control of my own rehabilitation. I had to try to do everything, even the improbable, to reach my full capability.

The National Institutes of Health conducted studies determining acupuncture to be a valuable medical therapy. While at the time hospitalization costs averaged $1,000 a day for mediocre treatment, I couldn't even get my doctor to write a prescription for a $65 acupuncture session. Massage was definitely out of the picture.

In China, injuries to the spine are treated at centers dedicated to a therapy called Chi Kung, an ancient practice of visualizing energy moving through your body. While not well known in America, Chi Kung does have its following, and a friend of mine who was an adherent to the practice brought her instructor, who was visiting

Hawaii, to see me. He had suffered multiple fractures to his spinal column in a car accident and credited his complete recovery to Chi Kung—eight hours of it a day, every day for a year.

Maybe the gutting of Medicare and Medicaid budgets will force the American government and society to consider other, less expensive medical models for complementary treatment. China's technological might is growing exponentially. Will East meet West in a symbiotic dance of mutual support? I'm betting on it; it's cost efficient.

A WALK IN THE PARK

The rehab hospital allowed me to use an old electric wheelchair on the weekends, which was great fun because I could finally go where I willed. A friend flew over from Maui one weekend to be the scheduled volunteer, and we decided to take a walk in the park across the street from the hospital. Aside from the shakedown cruise the physical therapist took me on to the local 7-11, this was my first outing in a power wheelchair. I felt confident in it and elated to get out of the hospital.

The park was one of these long, rambling, tree-shrouded oases adjacent to a stream. We were strolling down an old jogging path that paralleled the streambed. At one point, the asphalt path almost kissed the edge of a steep cliff above the stream. The dark snake of a path meandered within three feet of the precipice and was tilted due to erosion. There was a slanting dip ahead in my path and I remembered the instructions from the physical therapist: "If the road angles to one side, compensate by steering in the other direction—that way you will roll straight." I was rolling straight to catch up with my friend when I entered the dip. Following my instructions, I steered right to compensate the leftward sloping jogging path.

"Steer right" I thought, as I started to veer left.

"FULL RIGHT RUDDER!" I commanded under my breath as we turned to face the cliff's edge. As if the chair had a mind of its own and its mind was made up to commit suicide, it rolled slowly up to the edge—taking me with it! I began to call out to my friend but with my puny lung capacity, I could only whisper her name.

The front wheels of the chair had rolled within inches of the edge of the cliff. My feet were hovering over empty space. My eyes widened at the twenty-feet drop and the broken cinder blocks placed below to prevent further erosion.

Forget steering right, "FULL REVERSE!" I thought frantically, but this only slowed the march of the old chair, which insisted on being a lemming.

My friend was still some distance ahead, enjoying the oasis of the park in asphalt-covered Honolulu, and completely unaware of my dire situation.

I had given up. I was going over. A wash of surrender softened the muscles I could tense. I found myself once again in the grip of something larger than myself. Immediately, I felt as though I was back in the surf again, struggling for air, and then re-experiencing my stroke. Nothing could be done but to simply surrender, hoping I would survive the fall.

My eyes softened their focus and began to roll back into my head. I was slipping into a state of shock to avoid the oncoming pain. My friend's scream into my right ear brought me back into sharp focus. She had heard my plaintive cries, turned to see me inches from the edge and instantly exploded into a run for the chair. She grabbed onto the handles and for a few moments had a burst of adrenaline strength, but couldn't pull me back. She did prevent the rest of my front wheels from going over and her calls for help lifted a man recovering from leg surgery off a park bench to hobble to our rescue.

Once safe, I released my tension by crying. "What is happening? Is there a God and why is He doing this to me?" I thought.

The fall would have killed me. The 200-pound chair would have flipped over and sandwiched me on the broken cinder blocks below. Realizing this, all I could think about was that suddenly I wasn't safe outside. Everything was dangerous. Cars, dogs, even broken sidewalks could kill. In a crazed way, I actually began to conceive of the emotional torture chamber of the rehab hospital as a sanctuary, like a mother's bosom of safety and routine.

"Ok, that's it, I'm heading back," I concluded aloud. "Enough of the outside, it's too dangerous!"

But my wiser inner voice protested and said, "Michael, you have got to go on. You can't let this stop you. Fall off a horse, get back on. This is just the beginning of many challenges. Don't take them personally or else you'll get bitter and scared."

I came away from the experience with a deep appreciation for the fragility of life. As I continued to roll down the jogging path, I felt like I had just avoided years of therapy. By facing the big, bad world immediately after it nearly took my life, something profound gelled inside of me.

There was no reason to let fear control my life. That itself would be a living death. Even though I was in a wheelchair, I had to become more fully in charge of myself physically, emotionally and spiritually. There was nowhere to hide. I had to turn and face into the winds of adversity so I wouldn't get blown off balance.

I resolved to let every moment, every conversation, every thought, every breath, every walk in the park, become precious and worthy of full love and attention.

A MILE IN MY MOCCASINS

My friend and I returned to the hospital after our invigorating walk. I celebrated the seamless, flat floors and my friend decided to try on my moccasins. For the rest of the afternoon she commandeered a manual wheelchair and rolled around the hospital, immediately appreciating the strength needed to roll even on hard, flat surfaces. Forget about steps, even a slight slope was a major effort.

She was also amazed at how much attention was required just to avoid minor obstacles, and she found it impossible to carry on a conversation while negotiating a turn. But the most important realization was about the way staff members treated her.

She felt alone in a hospital filled with big people. Big not just because walking people tower over people in wheelchairs, but also because staff members avoided her eyes like she had the plague, which negated her existence.

I found that it was the little people, children, who were the first to come up and ask, "What happened?" and "Can I have a ride?" I also heard the elderly and those with obvious infirmities complain about big people looking right through them, as though they were invisible. Oh well.

THE EYES HAVE IT

I knew that feeling. None of the rehab personnel would look into my eyes. The doctor would flash a cursory glance my way while making a point, but then quickly go back to his notepad. The nurses would make eye contact if I was pleading a case about my treatment, but mostly they were there to mechanically perform a duty—to "do" me.

I was raised to pay the utmost attention to anyone with whom I converse by looking into the person's eyes. Doctors and nurses are in such close contact with so many people, I guess they just can't afford to connect with them all in this important way. Too bad, because ultimately I believe a sincere connection with the eyes enlivens people by showing respect and reflecting our souls to each other.

Unfortunately, after three weeks in the hospital I too began to avoid eye contact. So many staff people mechanically came in and out of my room that I just gave up. I relented and stared blankly up at the ceiling while they "did" me. Inflicting this subtle yet real emotional trauma on the newly injured and infirm is no way to run a rehab hospital.

Many hospitals are not emotionally healthy places to be. Why would some people be so afraid of others, simply because of their illnesses? "Doctors and nurses want to avoid getting personally involved with a patient who might die," defended one of my sisters, a thirty-year veteran of nursing. I can understand that, but will most people ripped out of their normal lives by illness or injury understand? Personally connecting with patients through eye contact, touch, a listening ear and the expression of sincere concern is as important as administering their medications and giving them food. No wonder visiting hours are so eagerly anticipated. That's when patients are able to share heartfelt and meaningful communication with someone.

Obviously there are exceptions. There are wonderful people working in our hospitals but as caseloads increase, personal time decreases. Medicine is in the clutches of being a bureaucracy completely run by the numbers. In my hospital experience, basic medical care was mediocre, therapy for a new quadriplegic was very poor and general nursing care was greatly diminished by the fact that 50 percent of the nurses couldn't fluently speak English. At least the food was surprisingly good.

Unfortunately, I spent seven awful weeks at the Russian Rehab Hospital of the xxxxxxx, but I'll spare you the rest of the details and go home.

Three months after my injury I flew home to Maui. At the house, friends had built access ramps and an outside shower with an ocean view. Navigating the airports threw me into shock—too many people moving too quickly. Even the drive home on a small country road seemed insanely fast. I keenly understood how fragile our little bodies really are.

3

A DAY IN THE LIFE

The most important routine of the day was exercise—or trying to fly.

This was a typical day in my neighborhood during the first few months following my injury. It began at eight o'clock in the morning when the nurse tiptoed into the house to awaken me. He or she would begin the bladder catheterization while I kept a black silk over my eyes, trying to drift back to a dream. Twenty minutes on, I was definitely awake because the nurse would be performing range-of-motion exercises on my legs, moving them in a series of spatial loops to trick the joints into self-lubrication. This was the time I would meditate and do breathing exercises. As long as the silk covered my eyes, the nurse wouldn't speak. As soon as I was blinking into the sunlight, however, the verbal barrage would begin.

During the rest of the morning, I would have a green protein drink and toast, a bed bath, and every third day orchestrate a bowel program. With clothes pulled on in bed, the final task was getting into the wheelchair using a Hoyer lift, said lift being modeled after the engine hoist used in garages. It was rather comical to see the nurse cranking the hydraulic handle, raising me off the bed like a dangling marionette. I was then dropped onto my nifty, new electric wheelchair and fluffed my clothes like a small child going to kindergarten.

At 11 a.m. there was a changing of the guards—nurse exit stage left, cue in volunteer du jour. From 11 a.m. to 5 p.m. every day, dear friends became surrogate hands and feet. They would prepare lunch, do catheterization, run errands (like cappuccinos and blueberry scones), help with paperwork, sweep the floors and do the wash. Essentially, they chopped wood and carried water.

Each volunteer had a specialty that graced my life—keeping up with my dictation on the computer, helping with finances and bookkeeping, researching therapies, masterful organizing, bringing videos, and scheduling the volunteers. One would come over to play devil's advocate, but we just ended up fighting. My friends' most crucial talent, however, was to see past my injury and recognize that I was just another normal guy.

Six o'clock p.m., sun low on the horizon, and in came the night shift. Two other people lived in the house and I paid their rent in exchange for several evenings of caregiving per week. One was a registered nurse, who showed up four nights a week with groceries or the other fruits of my many errands. After dinner, we would do the nightly rituals of cathing, bedding, exercising, medicating, and *Star Trek* watching. In addition to his night duties, he was an official chore worker. I could count on him to keep the house running like a well-oiled machine. He was completely dedicated to my recovery and I truly feel he was heaven-sent.

My other housemate was a twenty-something athletic trainer who hailed from Massachusetts. She had just landed on Maui and her mother, who was visiting, painted her room and hung frilly curtains; good for mothers.

One of the night shift duties was to get up at 3 a.m. to help me turn over for pressure relief, cath me and trade interrupted dreams. I had not yet had a complete, uninterrupted night's sleep since my injury, which fostered conditions for epic dreaming. Everything took on an air of mythic importance. I felt like my subconscious was birthing a new life, and that that life was slowly percolating up into my day-to-day reality.

BE HERE NOW

Good morning! Dream time over. It was 8 a.m. and a nurse opened the screen door for the routine to begin all over again.

An artist friend commented to me once that my life in those early days seemed rather similar to that of Sisyphus, the Greek god who would heave a heavy boulder up a mountain only to have it roll back down again. Because Sisyphus chose to be an active, conscious participant of this repetitive, laborious cycle, he was engaged in and yet above the tedium. I too was fully engaged with my rock and mountain. In the midst of recurring, day-to-day cycles, I would experience moments of euphoria and heart-opening tenderness. These magical moments kept me going like breadcrumbs in the woods, directional beacons leading me onward. Many of these epiphanies came when I wasn't *doing* anything. Sneaking up from behind, a wave of *being* would wash over me. I then had the time and freedom to be completely engaged with watching clouds stream overhead or a train of ants scurry along a railing below.

In these timeless moments, long forgotten memories began seeping back into my daily consciousness. Once, all of a sudden I was twelve years old again, hidden in the branches of my favorite climbing tree. My senses were exquisitely alive and accessible: I was flooded by the sound of rustling leaves, the touch of tree bark beneath my hands and the sight of the green and blue canopy overhead. This and other immersions into the best of my early years all were food for my soul.

Recalling these memories from my youth led me to conceive of my injury as a rebirthing experience. I even bought a baby book; you know, the scrapbooks that list milestones—first feeding, first diaper change, first bath, first outing in a carriage, first word, first cup of coffee—all the big events that mark growth stages in life. I remained fascinated by how well the analogy of being reborn applied to my post-injury new life, only (thankfully) the second time around I got to relive my youth with the consciousness of a forty-something-year-old.

I'M GETTIN' BETTAH ALL THE TIME

I continued with daily physical therapy and gained increasing control over my arms. One return of sensation was in the very center of my finger pads. This small area became surprisingly alive with sensation. I could gently bite my index finger and send electric ripples throughout my upper body.

A Chinese herbalist was helping me improve my nutrition, so I was getting all the vitamins and supplements I'd ever want, but far too many yucky, unrecognizable powders, teas and salves. All of this, combined with getting over ten hours of sleep per night, made me feel healthier and more vital than I had in years.

Not that I didn't waver some. I was humbled by bladder infections and bouts of feeling anxious and depressed, like I was on the edge with my toes hanging over the abyss. Those were the times when I would try to do one creative thing, sometimes as simple as straightening a book on my desk. One of my favorite creative acts to stop the feedback loop of depression was refining and redefining my living environment—I got into feathering my nest.

VIRTUAL VEHICLE

For many wheelers, the computer became a viable way to virtually explore the world. The Internet was just exploding and it was the golden age... before we got spammed.

An astronaut friend, Commander Gerald Carr, and his artist wife Pat gave me a gift that allowed me to wander the world at will—a powerful computer, which I loaded with adaptive equipment. Voice activation software had finally matured into a reliable method for entering text into the computer by speech alone. A state-of-the art program listened to my voice and took dictation. In order to train it in the nuances of my vocal personality, I had to read a predetermined script for about an hour. Then, all of a sudden, I could write whenever the urge struck!

Because my fingers didn't function, a regular mouse was replaced with a head mouse. A small, reflective sticker was attached to the corner of my reading glasses. This dot reflected an infrared beam coming from a box on top of my monitor so that wherever my head moved, the cursor on the screen obediently followed. I still had to click something, so on my desk sat a big purple button I could whack with my wrist.

These wonderful friends from Arkansas gave me the world with this magical machine. By providing me with a virtual vehicle, they single handedly kept me from sinking into the isolation of extreme boredom. I took to the technological wonder like a sixteen-year-old boy takes to a '65 Mustang, with a new driver's license pressed into that little plastic window of his wallet.

GOODNESS GRACIOUS... GREAT TIRES AFIRE

It's hard to believe time can fly by when you're sitting still. My days had been filled with time-consuming routines yet in retrospect, the weeks and months after my injury flew by. The two-year window of dramatic healing was beginning to close.

A spinal cord injury can become so deeply inflamed it chokes off nerve impulses like a severe ankle sprain. It can take up to two years for the inflammation to go down and allow signals to pass freely through undamaged nerves. I felt an urgent need to get on with the healing process, but traditional healing therapies couldn't be done in Hawaii. Our only rehab hospital was like an exhausted, third world institution. My only chance was to go to the mainland.

But I couldn't travel until I'd secured my foundation. I had a house, food supply, basic healthcare and the support of friends, but no personal transportation! A special county van for the elderly and disabled would take me to doctors' appointments, but otherwise I was trapped in my monastery. Perhaps being Monk Michael was part of the Grand Plan, but nonetheless, it was time for a van.

I spent nine months entrenched in the planning—I made dozens of phone calls, compared *Blue Book* values, attacked every Sunday paper "Classifieds" section, researched camper tops, nailed down an appropriate chairlift and hardest of all, decided on a paint color for the van. This and much more went into giving birth to a vehicle that could get me out of the house. I located a good, used workhorse at last and shipped it over to Honolulu for retrofitting into a wheelchair van. Because everyone was working on "Hawaii time", I didn't get it back for two months. Finally, the day arrived and my wheelchair van rolled off the barge from Honolulu. It was a Friday. I opened a bottle of champagne with a group of friends and toasted my freedom.

The van complemented my nifty new $20,000 electric wheelchair (thank you, Medicaid). The chair allowed me to travel around my property alone, without fear of getting stuck, while the van let me stay in my power wheelchair to travel around the island and experience bits of wilderness. I was so tired of seeing the same walls day after day. House arrest wasn't much better than being in prison. A change of pace and scenery would be great. I owned a van!

Since I could finally get out and experience the world spontaneously, the next morning a volunteer and I jumped into the van on a whim to go to the movies. It was a deep-in-my-soul thrill to just pick up and go without the hassles of being physically manhandled into and out of a regular car. I sat proudly in my van, which had taken nine months to birth. Everything from the air conditioner to the chairlift was in top condition. I was a beaming papa!

I rolled into the theater and took my place in the crummy wheelchair stall (why are they always in the back, with the floor sloped to one side?). The previews had just ended when the manager tapped me on the shoulder and whispered, "Uhhh, I think your van is on fire."

BACK IN THE SURF AGAIN

Many hands held open the doors to the movie theater. I put my chair into high gear and scooted across the parking lot to my smoking van. A policeman kept me at a safe distance, while I watched the paint peel and listened to the hiss of air conditioner coolant escaping. Déjà vu. I was back in the surf, having a stroke, and on the edge of the cliff again, but instead of seeing my life flash before my eyes, I saw the next three months of van repair hassles and house arrest.

Under the flashing lights, while the firemen did their duty, I sat staring in front of the smoldering carcass of my new friend. Within seconds, I'd glimpsed the future. I knew the fire had totaled the van, but the added accessibility equipment would be okay. I would have to find the same make and model in order to somehow transfer my adaptive equipment. The insurance would be a hassle, a replacement van would be hard to locate, I would be under house arrest for at least another three months and worst of all, I'd have to choose another color.

When I saw the tow truck backing up to mate with my van, I suddenly realized I didn't have a way to get home! I needed an accessible van with a wheelchair lift and the county vans didn't run on weekends. My volunteer wasn't trained to transfer me into a taxi and besides, I couldn't leave a $20,000, 250-pound wheelchair abandoned on the side of the road. Surprisingly, I was calm and confident that I would be supported in my emergency; after all, something that horrible just couldn't exist without its opposite nearby.

CALLING ALL ANGELS

He was in his mid-fifties, worked construction at the new mall and had a police scanner in his truck. In the midst of the whirl of firemen, policemen, tow truck drivers and the merely curious, this man meekly caught my attention and whispered, "I have a van that can take you home." His son had multiple sclerosis and he offered to go home and get his converted van.

We squished inside the tiny minivan as twilight swirled around the parking lot. In my whole life, I had never felt so lost. Until this gentle man came up with the answer, I had no idea how to get home with my wheelchair. This living "on the edge" was getting to me. Back under house arrest, I felt more depressed than at any time since my injury.

"OK, this has to be for a reason," I yelled aloud. "A fire twenty minutes into my new van has to mean something. What's the flipside to this coin?" I didn't bother to search for an answer. I gave up for the day, turned on the television and drank three beers.

GET YOUR STORY OUT AND THEY WILL COME

The next morning, a reporter from the local newspaper called, wanting to do a story about my van fire. She ended up writing a terrific account for a front page article featuring a color photo of me hitchhiking in my wheelchair. The title caption read "Calling All Angels."

Within days, the mailman had delivered enough in donations to fund the transfer of my adaptive equipment to another van. Many mechanics offered to help repair the damage and out of the blue appeared—another van! The article had opened Maui's heart. The community gave me the means to repair my burnt van and donated a second one for interim transportation. Unfortunately, it was very old and not long for this world, but it would get me out of the house during the three months needed to repair my toasted vehicle.

My donated second vehicle was a cavernous, retired airport shuttle. Up to eight people, plus my wheelchair, could pile in and go to the beach, a movie or a fire sale.

The article ran ten days before a benefit to raise money for my advanced therapy on the mainland. The added publicity swelled the attendance and the gala, held in the ballroom of the largest hotel on Maui, was a sweeping success! Four bands donated their music and two hundred and forty Mauian angels donated their goods and services to a catalog of items for sale that evening. Since the event was held on my birthday, the big heart rush came when everyone sang "Happy Birthday" holding hands in a circle around me. With deep appreciation for my huge extended family, I slowly spun around to look each person in the eye.

At the end of the night, I tallied enough donations to get me within spitting distance of an innovative therapy center for the paralyzed. Although it looked disastrous at the time, because of the fire I ended up with a better quality van, a second van to give to another Maui wheeler, the ability to go to the next level of therapy and a total belief in angels.

I read a nice idea once that angels are the eaters of darkness. Nothing exists without its opposite. When surrounded by the fires of life's traumas, I came to know the faint, cooling breeze of angel wings upon my cheeks.

CALIFORNIA ON MY MIND

Located in Irvine, California, in beautiful Orange County, the Petrofsky Center was where I hoped to go for my next stage of healing. But in order to get there, I would have to go out into the big, bustling world of walking people, a prospect that at the time seemed kind of scary. I'd gotten used to my protective routine and dreaded its disruption (for fear that something bad might happen). I found new compassion for the elderly, understanding their fear of change and harm coming to them from outside their secure, known worlds. Daily, I had to forcibly expand an ever contracting comfort zone.

Anticipating I would be a nervous wreck for the first few days in California, I eagerly hoped that "grace" would kick in. I don't believe we're asked to face a fear and are then left empty-handed to go through the experience. In each challenge, we have untapped resources ready to be claimed for the first time. In Catholic theology, this support is known as grace, a gift of the Spirit. It's like free bonus mileage to help us in our travels throughout life.

RAINDROPS KEEP FALLING ON MY HEAD

The seven very large pieces of luggage checked in for my flight to Los Angeles were an awesome sight. I tried to keep my stuff to a minimum, but it seemed I needed everything, from the air mattress to sleep on to the box carrying my backup wheelchair. My caregiver had boxed up his ten-speed bicycle. We were off to see the wizard.

I had traded in all my mileage coupons for a first class upgrade. Flying coach didn't seem possible because I thought my special, pressure-relieving air cushion would be too wide for the seats. Boarding the plane in front of the other four hundred travelers was great and flying first class was a delight. The stewardess invited my caregiver to join me from coach and take the empty seat next to mine. At midnight, we touched down on our first destination—LAX.

The Super Shuttle driver filled us in on the news that massive rains had just rolled through the area. I couldn't afford to rent a wheelchair van for my month-long stay, so I'd booked a hotel within rolling distance of the Petrofsky Center. "Smart," I thought. "It's just four blocks."

Long blocks, I discovered—totaling a mile, in fact. The winter storms flooding California were in fact still raging, but my caregiver devised the perfect solution for staying dry. I donned a green, hooded poncho that covered most of my electric chair and pulled large garbage bags up over my legs, protecting them from the rain. I rolled to the center on rain-soaked streets fast enough to keep my caregiver at a jogging pace behind me. To the cars zooming past us, I probably looked like an antiquated, Eastern European military tank on maneuvers, with the infantry following behind. But I never got soaked and enjoyed the daily fresh air.

BACK TO THE FUTURE

After nine months of researching therapy centers, Petrofsky had come out on top. During my month-long program at the center, I would get a complete, detailed assessment of my condition, which would then be a baseline for further improvement. Biofeedback would indicate even the faintest of pulses getting through to my muscles. Electro-stimulation would exercise muscles I'd not used since my injury. Computers would control the electro-stim to my legs in a regulated fashion, so that I could work out by pedaling a stationary bicycle. I would come away with an exercise/therapy program that would maintain my body at optimum levels so I would be ready when the "cure" came along.

Leading medical authorities agreed it wasn't *if*, but *when* for the development of a cure. So even if I didn't overcome paralysis on my own, I would stay in good shape waiting for traditional medicine to come up with the answers.

THE GREAT FROG LEG EXPERIMENT

My time at the Petrofsky Center held my first experience with other wheelers and I was very intimidated. Up until then, I had been a wheeler in a normal world and felt it was just a matter of time until I rejoined the walkers. Suddenly I was in "their" world, spending eight hours a day in a culture that I didn't want to accept. They traded stories of falling from wheelchairs, catheters, frustration over limited access, inadequate healthcare, bed sores and financial travails and I was forced to listen. Acceptance of my new relatives came hard and I had to swallow it.

But these wheelchair veterans were also living life to the fullest. They drove their own cars, went snow skiing, played quad rugby (that fellow always had bruised knuckles), got married and lived "normal" lives. I still saw myself as a walker someday, yet realized from the courage of these wheelers that whatever happened to me, I could still be happy and fulfilled.

Dr. Petrofsky's clinic sat in a suburban, industrial area of Irvine, in what looked to be a former dance studio. Mirrors lined the walls and equipment crowded the floors. The clinic also housed the doctor's exotic workshops, where he designed and created electro-stim machines and other therapy devices from scratch. He was the leading researcher on functional-electro-stimulation, or F.E.S. The "functionality" came from wiring people up to stimulate the proper muscles so they could exercise on various machines. His crowning achievement was assisting paraplegics to walk again, using waist-mounted computers, walkers and leg braces.

My first day at the clinic was the last for a seventeen-year-old girl who'd been injured in a car crash. Dr. Petrofsky had her walking across the room while he adjusted the tiny computer strapped to her waist. She later commented to me that she thought her accident was one of the better things that had ever happened in her life. I choked up and couldn't ask why. I choke up a lot when I see the human spirit at its best. I assumed, like many spinal cord injured, that she was closer to family and friends than ever before and her focus on life was clearer, concentrated on living each day to its full potential.

My time at the clinic was easy. I just sat there while my caregiver did all the work. He would move the electro-pads among the ten muscle groups needing exercise, then turn the power dial up and down every ten seconds. This procedure took thirty minutes per muscle group. He learned how to lapse into a Zen-like state of mind. I learned how to take catnaps sitting up.

I touted the Petrofsky Center as being a leading edge therapy clinic, but in my opinion electro-stimulation should be part of the basic exercise routine prescribed for any spinal cord injured person. Every wheeler leaving the hospital should be sent home with electro-stim equipment and a stand-up frame, two indispensable treatment modalities for maintaining bone strength and muscle mass. Unfortunately, the bureaucracies of traditional medicine and insurance companies consider these treatments excessive and would rather save money in the near term only to spend much more money in the long term for broken bones, bed sores and damaged feet from poor circulation.

My caregiver and I left the Petrofsky clinic with an electro-stim unit I purchased for home use. I could already see muscles that had been dormant taking shape beneath my skin. We raided the clinic's library, voraciously learning about other therapies I saw in my future and photocopying vast amounts of information for later reference. My physical stamina had dramatically increased from my time at the clinic, which was good, because we were off to the next adventure—a week long, eighteen hours a day seminar experience intended to reframe the paradigm of business.

This new business model aimed for movement from competition to cooperation, from following the crowd to following your heart and passion. After my injury, I realized I had a new life that I could consciously form, and all the fingers of fate had pointed to this seminar. I didn't want to resume work as an hourly wage earner. I wanted to work as part of a like-minded team, concocting meaningful projects that would bring multiple income streams for years to come.

I was excited to have my sister from Kansas City join me on this adventure. This was the first time in our adult lives that we'd spent time together away from other family members. Within one week, we remembered the love we had for each other as children, while coming to a new respect for each other's adult wisdom.

This was also the first time I was around a large group of strangers when I wasn't 6'6" in standing height, but 5'3" having taken a seat. All these huge people milled about and couldn't see me until they stumbled and looked down. I felt like an alley cat, scurrying wide-eyed to safer locations.

What a shift! I missed being able to look over people's heads in a crowd. I had my sister run interference for me as we wove through pockets of incredibly big people. The other attendees were great, however, and eventually developed a sixth sense to the motor noise of my presence. By the end of the week, my alley cat persona had been melted away by human warmth, kindness and sensitivity.

EXIT TO EDEN

The conference completed our stay in California. I left with heightened enthusiasm and a stockpile of new ideas. On departure, however, while boarding the plane for Maui, I suddenly got worried. First class was totally full, so my caregiver would have to stay in his coach seat. I would have to completely fend for myself for the first time since my injury. Food and drink would be a challenge. I still felt awkward struggling in public and in case of turbulence, really didn't want to fall over sideways onto a stranger's lap.

As it turned out, the flight crew came up with a strap to secure me to my seat. And the stranger in the next seat was sitting on some feathers. A wife and mother from the horse country of Pennsylvania graciously took me under her wing for the five-hour flight back home to paradise. She helped me with food, drink, headphones and even magazines.

Whenever I was enveloped in fear that something would go wrong, or I wouldn't have enough, or my van would run out of gas, or a host of other concerns, I remembered my Dad's advice: "Don't worry, things will always work out."

Angels will be beside me, I will always have enough and my van will always reach the gasoline pumps. My constant lesson is to trust that this adventure is purposeful and I will always be supported, even when life gets funny.

4

FUNNY MONEY

This chapter is dedicated to all the disabled and elderly people in America
struggling to maintain their quality of life.

Although we live in the wealthiest country on the planet, the disabled and the elderly are forced to make do with less and less, and accept the role of "warehoused people." While I felt that I was in better shape than most, I hope my story puts a personal face to the abstract budget numbers that scroll across the evening news. Here's what I looked like fiscally in 1995.

Facts of Life (monthly income)

$450 from Social Security used for housing

$400 from state of Hawaii used for evening care

$350 from computer work used for evening care

$100 from state of Hawaii in food stamps

The state also covered my van insurance.

Medicare paid for basic medical insurance.

Medicaid covered four hours a day of nursing assistance.

Said nursing assistance would begin at 7 a.m. I was exercised, boweled, bathed, dressed, and in the chair by 10 a.m. Then I'd have breakfast and technically be on my own until 7 p.m., when a paid evening caregiver would arrive.

Friends would volunteer their time to me each day between 2 and 6 p.m. We lunched, cleaned house, exercised, got mail, put order to my desk and ran errands.

Evening caregivers came in from 7 to 9 p.m. to help with dinner, getting into bed, more exercising, taking evening medications, setting me up for sleep and cleaning house. These noble helpers were also available overnight in case of emergency—and I could only afford to pay them $32 per twelve-hour shift.

I shared a house with the office of my former working buddies. Because of the shared rent, I was able to live and work in a larger home. This setup also ensured backup assistance throughout the day, plus I had the added benefit of comradeship, which helped to avoid feeling like a shut-in.

Augustus Horribilis

The first year and a half of my new life had been spent stabilizing myself physically and mentally in a new environment. Life was a daily effort to make ends meet. Ready or not, I had to start earning money to pay for my evening care.

My state benefits covered only half of my evening care, because benefits in Hawaii were given with the assumption that the disabled lived with blood family, who could shoulder the bulk of their care. Since my Hawaii family was only of the extended variety, I had to hire people to cover the missing half. Only months before my injury, benefits to the disabled ensured full evening care, but state budget cutbacks had dramatically reduced this coverage. Going back to limited work was the obvious way to cover the other half. So in August, I started earning money again.

Concurrently, I had waves of sensation returning to my right leg. In addition to the gentle tingling of leg hairs against the inside of my pants, deep, tectonic stresses were coming to my attention as searing pain. These sensations were as debilitating as they were curiously welcome. My muscles were telling me they were under duress.

"Pay attention now Michael, you don't want to damage the legs that you'll walk on someday," they screamed.

"You aren't doing enough, Kanouff. Here—try ignoring this pain—like a red hot ice pick sizzling into your hip socket."

My whole life stopped, and my new profession was to be a pain manager.

Thus began my search to discover what was causing the pain and how to manage said demon. It had reached the two Percocet pain pill level and was climbing. My doctor had no idea about its cause and just suggested taking stronger pain medication. Funds were not available for any other types of treatment, so it was up to me to play detective.

I tried various massage techniques and positioning in bed with differing pillow supports. I could also lie flat in my articulating wheelchair to relieve pressure on my lower back, hips and legs. I even pulled out my industrial strength electro-stimulation machines and performed the famous high school biology class frog experiment. High-voltage electrodes were taped onto my leg muscles to make them jump on their own. The idea was to increase muscle mass for extra cushioning. Unfortunately, however, the treatments only caused my pain to go ballistic.

Many "alternative healers" visited my home, but no miracles occurred. Even a state-supplied physical therapist was given one hour a week for a month to figure out the cause of my pain. She left me with three photocopied pages of stick figures doing range-of-motion techniques and suggested using a heating pad. Oh well. I realized then that pain management was solely up to me.

I felt alone at first, isolated with my pain and with nowhere to go. Yet when I knew that I was totally responsible for my health, something changed inside. I became empowered. Of course I would see doctors, nurses and pharmacists but they were now my assistants, my staff. They were my hired hands to follow up on ideas I'd discovered on the Internet or in speaking with other wheelers. I was in charge of myself and it felt great!

August also began the search for a new house, because the lease would be up in November. While it would've been nice to move with my working group, who provided friendship, assistance and an in-house job, a house to fit all our requirements was painfully hard to find. To top it all off, my live-in caregiver gave his two-week notice.

FIRE IN THE HOLD

I was alone, working on my computer. My volunteer for the day had a scheduling conflict, so I was "toughing it out" that afternoon. The nurse had fixed a protein smoothie that morning to get me by until the evening caregiver shift began at 7 p.m. The afternoon promised to be a quiet time for writing. At around 2:30, the phone rang.

Shifting both my gaze and hand toward the phone, my body went stupid and I lost control of my movement. My hand careened past the phone, hitting a stack of papers. My head started spinning and I got very disoriented. I had just enough time to throw the chair into the layback position. I fought to stay conscious as my blood pressure dropped and my vision of the ceiling clouded.

While going down, I called out to a friend working in the adjacent office to come quickly.

"My God, I'm having another stroke!" I thought.

Once down, I couldn't talk, only gesture and grunt. Thankfully, my friend understood "911" and I was off to the emergency room. All the way down the hill, I sobbed. Everything looked dark in my life. I felt doomed. The pressure of "holding it all together" was relieved only by willfully, completely surrendering to this immovable force that had me in its grip—yet again.

The ambulance attendant tried to console me. Because I still had difficulty speaking, I couldn't explain that the tears were welcome; I was glad for them. Sinking so deeply into my emotions was catalyzing something within me, I was sure of that. My emotional meltdown would set the stage for something more magnificent to crystallize in my life. It had to. (Does a caterpillar cry when it's dying in the process of becoming a butterfly?)

Déjà vu. I ended up in the same ER stall where I'd been taken two and a half years ago, after my beach injury! The ceiling looked so familiar. I started to cry again. My blood was tested and I was pumped full of antibiotics. I had a raging, painful bladder infection. I couldn't fully feel the depth of the physical pain, but it did affect me emotionally, hence the intense tears. The infection was severe enough to cause a dramatic drop in blood pressure, which temporarily mimicked a stroke. Gradually, my speech returned and I could talk to the friends standing vigil around me. My blood pressure was stabilized and I was sent home at 3 a.m.

For the next day and a half, I cried constantly. Without someone else having been in the house, I could have suffered alone, flirting with a catastrophic stroke for three hours, until the arrival of my evening caregiver. I was also emotionally sensitive because of the bladder infection and psychologically drained due to the number of no-win situations in my life that had led me to the breaking point.

HUD-R-US

Two days prior, I had been called in for my first appointment with HUD—the United States Department of Housing and Urban Development. In addition to rebuilding urban centers, this arm of the government underwrites the rent of the needy. In my state, there was usually a five-year wait after making application. Due to my severely limited income, I was able to cut in line after a two and a half year wait; more than 50 percent of my income went to pay rent.

I was more than just excited. I was greatly relieved. Finally, I would get some financial help from our government for housing. The previous thirty months had been a real challenge to make ends meet. I was willing to do my share in partnership with family, community and government. I knew that with all of us working together, I could stay out of the dreaded nursing home (which, by the way, was exponentially more expensive than home care).

The morning of the first HUD meeting I was very excited. I finally got to the office and was brusquely informed that all they could offer was a certificate for studio housing. The rent could be no more than $750 a month, they would only cover 75 percent of that amount, and I would have to live alone! No office and no housemates (although they would allow one roommate as a caregiver?). My caseworker proudly declared that the studio would have to meet HUD's construction criteria and then added, "I do the site inspection and fail 40 percent of them."

Stammering from the stunning news, I explained my need as a single quadriplegic to have a home with extra bedrooms for housemate caregivers. "Could I at least use the subsidy to go in with others on a larger house?" I pleaded. "That way I could have people around in case of emergency, and the common rooms would be large enough for my wheelchair."

The caseworker brusquely retorted, "That's the 'Voucher Program' and it's closed. We only have the 'Certificate Program' open and only studios are available for you."

He presented a stack of papers for me to sign and then gave the coup de gras. I had two months to find a studio that would pass inspection or else I'd be thrown back into the recertification process.

"You must also come up with the security deposit," the HUD man said. "We used to do that, but not any more."

HUD refused to allow their money to go into a larger, shared house, so I'd have to live alone in a small studio apartment! On Maui, that meant less floor space than a trailer home. I thought it still might be possible though, if I found a small, cheap, two-bedroom house, one in which I could get my large chair through the bedroom door.

A series of scenarios started firing through my brain. "Should I move into a tiny house with one other person who might not be able to bear the total load of my care? One evening caregiver alone might burn out within a few months, but if I got a second, they'd have to sleep on the living room floor. Can I tough it out? I wouldn't have the security of living in a house bustling with friends and colleagues during the day, but would have many more hours alone, a blessing and a curse. Or should I decline the HUD subsidy and remain living with friends, even though it would be a financial struggle?"

I completely understood that every HUD regulation was born in response to abuse of the system. My caseworker had had his caseload increased until there was only time to see his clients as numbers. Any deviation from normal procedure was a time-consuming irritant. The numeralization of individuals is only one sad outcome of a diminishing governmental commitment to social service programs. On the nightly news, they call this phenomenon "increasing budget constraints."

I was coming to understand the new world of bureaucracy in my life. It was much like a dance, actually; a tango of love and hate, and I had to learn to follow the rules to get what I wanted. I hated being a case number, but was relieved to get the help that I received—if I didn't dance on anyone's toes. "I can do this," I thought. "It will be hard to swallow my pride, but I need this financial and medical support. OK. What's next?"

WILL THAT BE CHECK OR CHARGE?

For a couple of years, my new life had been bolstered by a band of friends and their in-house business. Before and after my injury we all shared a large house on a Maui beach as both an office and a home. It sat on a small cliff overlooking the vast Pacific Ocean. In the winter we could see migrating whales.

Maui had no public transportation system, so living at my workplace was the way to go. By working with adaptive devices, I'd boosted my computer skills to 50 percent of my previous capacity. My part-time monthly earnings averaged $200-$350 a month.

In December, at my year-end Medicaid/food stamp reauthorization meeting, my caseworker coolly informed me that I had been in error. Because of my new computer income, my food stamps would be reduced from $195 to $100 per month.

"You also have to pay us back for the last five months of overpayment," he demanded. "That comes to $475. How do you want to pay for this?

For two and a half years after my injury, I lived and worked just a few feet from the ocean. I'd gone snorkeling in that water, gathering up the golf balls my stupid neighbor sliced and hooked into the ocean just for fun. I reported him.

Two weeks later, I was posed that same question by my Social Security caseworker. Because of my meager new income, I was disqualified from receiving my Supplemental Security Income payments of $40 a month. She also asked how I intended to repay the money ($200). I could understand their logic, but I could feel the desperate financial pressures in my life.

Both accepted a $10 per month payment plan.

Downsizing

The following April, I was informed that Medicaid budget cuts would affect my nursing care. It was called "downsizing." Medicaid funding cuts at the top "trickled down", creating pressure all the way to the bottom, to me. Someone decided that hiring nurses for home care was too expensive, so in one swathe of a pen, dozens of RNs on Maui were terminated. "Oh, you can work, but you'll be paid on the home health aide pay scale," echoed over their telephone wires.

Since most of the nurses were independent contractors, they had no recourse—no union for a strike or negotiations and thus no work. My nurse had a mortgage payment and a family to support, so she quit working on Maui and flew over to another island for four days a week of killer shifts. Her two young boys would have to be raised by a nanny. Other RNs just gave up and moved to the mainland.

Because it wasn't "in the budget," no replacement home health aides could come in on my nurse's last day to be trained in my care. It wasn't rocket science, but learning the detailed routine that had taken so long for me to develop gave me the best shot at not aggravating my painful leg.

Please understand what a sublime torture it was to train new people every day in the subtleties of my care. At the end of three hours, my brain would be fatigued from giving direction every thirty seconds and my leg would scream from the novice care.

Since home health aides were in great demand after the downsizing, they were in short supply and shuffled around the island. I would train a new aide one day only to have another stranger wake me up from sleep the next to say, "Hi, I'm your aide, Bob. What do I do?" April began a mind-numbing period of adjustment.

Since home health aides received only six weeks of training, they weren't allowed to dispense medication. They could open prescription bottles, hold them in front of me so I could confirm their contents and squeeze them into the clenched grip of my right hand. Then I would lift each bottle to my lips and fish out the correct number of pills with my tongue. I would have up to fourteen pills scheduled each morning and handing the bottles back, I always felt demeaned and angry. State Medicaid administrators myopically expected blood family to administer prescriptions and thus assume liability... yet another crack through which I fell.

PENNY SAVED, DOLLAR LOST

Ever since the social service cutbacks of the 80s, I'd seen report after report pronouncing abstract figures of budget cuts. Many of today's homeless people used to be in hospitals for the mentally ill that were closed. If human life is so precious that abortion centers can be bombed, how dare we let another person freeze in a packing crate down some dark alley? The dignity of human life in need should take precedence over a $25,000 tax cut incentive to purchase an SUV.

In my opinion, Social Security, Medicaid and Medicare funding should never be cut, particularly from children's services and basic healthcare for the elderly and disabled. My cuts were minimal compared to those of other people on assistance, but we all faced continued "devaluation." I came to know firsthand what the moving of a decimal point can do to people's lives.

Cases in point...

My state-run Medicaid dental program sent a letter saying they were cutting all dental services except emergency care. If I were to have an abscess, I would have to see a preauthorized Medicaid provider. Oh, by the way, dentists on Maui weren't accepting Medicaid—the payments were too low. So with my jaw inflamed and in severe pain, I would've had to fly to Honolulu for treatment. They were willing to cover the cost of two round trip airplane tickets and two round trip taxi fares, all to see a dentist on the program that agreed to their low payment.

The state ran the only hospital on Maui and legislators had frozen the budget for permanent nursing staff. Since the facility was already way understaffed, as the caseload rose, they were forced to hire temporary nurses at twice the cost! Or, nurses were flown in from Honolulu and housed for a three-day work stint.

After desperate research, I discovered that my leg pain could be reduced to a manageable level with a specific, deep tissue massage. After two and half years of sitting on my leg muscles, they had knotted up from lack of circulation and spasms. Medicaid would gladly pay for expensive pain killers, but as my case nurse said, "Don't even think of getting a prescription for therapeutic massage from Medicaid."

Thankfully, my extended family was loaded with professional massage therapists who volunteered time to my leg, but what about other wheelers who didn't have support? They were forced to live with intense pain, in a mind-numbing cloud of painkillers, under the curse of being "warehoused." Medicaid rules were so strict and unbendable, they couldn't respond to a situation that would save them money in the long run. Isn't that curious?

Medicare decided not to pay for rubber gloves, so caregivers had to wash their hands in lieu of using sterile gloves when they cleaned my catheter. Often, they did an inadequate job washing up. Since the catheter was a known highway to the bladder for bacteria, Medicare ended up paying more for treating bladder infections than preventing them with boxes of gloves.

I deeply appreciated my government's support, yet I regret that we as a people don't fund Medicaid, Medicare or even Social Security to do more than just keep people alive. Preventive care could pull so many people out of an expensive, degenerative, downward spiral. It could pull them out of pain and despair and restore them to a society filled with promise and success.

SORRY

A week following my trip to the ER to fight the bladder infection, a nurse was inserting a new catheter into my bladder and I erupted in blood. Off to the ER again, but at least I avoided an overnight hospital stay.

The next morning my home health aide didn't show up at the usual time of 7 a.m. to help me get up. I lay quietly until 8:30, thinking there was a scheduling mix-up. The morning sun was pounding through the window and began to cook me under the quilt. Without the professional courtesy of a phone call, I had to assume the aide was a no show. Realizing I had to act quickly, I recruited my housemate to be late for his day job and just throw me in the chair. It was a thirty-minute process, a sloppy shortcutting of my normal three-hour procedure. My head throbbed from the previous night's bloodletting adventure and my leg burned from the morning's hasty get up.

I learned from making a subsequent phone call to the healthcare agency that I wasn't guaranteed an aide every day—"Sorry." If they couldn't fill a shift, then I was supposed to have a blood family member or another primary caregiver step in and do all the work. The agency considered their home health aides to be supplemental; they were only meant to come in and give a break, a respite, to primary caregivers. Not living with blood family, my funds went to hiring housemates for evening care, so I didn't have anyone as backup for mornings, except the state-supplied aides.

That morning I was on my own.

My clothes were crooked, my body unwashed and my face unshaven. I was given a pile of cookies on my lap to hold me for the day. I looked in the mirror and felt like a homeless person was staring back at me. I took the shambles of the morning and made lemonade. I went outside!

To heck with everything screaming for my attention inside the house, I was going out exploring. For two and a half years, I'd rarely been up in the chair early enough to see the delicate morning light. As a photographer I lived for the morning and late afternoon light. To be out in it again left me swooning.

I rolled around my little subdivision drinking up the morning's warm, soft glow. The tropical colors on houses and lush, green foliage came alive in these timeless moments. This ecstasy was the closest to God consoling me that I'd felt in a long time. The experience recharged my soul just as I was about to slip into a dark hole of bitterness and cynicism.

DAWN WITHIN THE DARKEST

I ended my tour by just sitting in the driveway, serenely watching the world go by. I noticed a dancing light on the pavement, a tinkerbell that would shimmer only within the shadow of a telephone pole. A "For Sale" sign was flopping in the wind, reflecting the sun onto the pavement. This special light was invisible except within the relative darkness of the shadow of the telephone pole.

What a perfect metaphor for having a vision of sublime light during our darkest hours. I don't think we are given dark, dire events in our lives without corresponding opportunities for growth. Sometimes we have to be enveloped by a shroud of darkness in order to see the subtle, shimmering gifts of grace and beauty within our reach. After all, diamonds are born in dark furnaces, catalyzed by mountains of pressure.

For me, when life was at its darkest, I learned that I had to make a conscious choice to reach out of a bitter, despondent mood with an act of love. One sincere compliment, one small easing of another's burden, one selfless gesture could start in motion a magical chain of events.

This magic included the most important act of love—loving myself! I gave myself the gift of "Morning Light" and it set in motion a cascade of events that changed my whole week. The most important thing I had to do in my new life was to learn how to love myself more and give to myself a quality of life that I didn't have before my injury

5

COLORS OF THE DAY

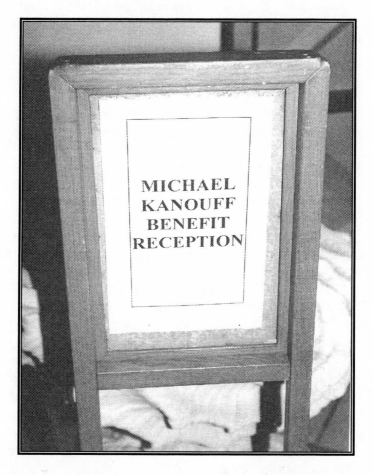

Community support was essential to being able to travel to the mainland for advanced therapy. Throwing a benefit was the best way to get the needed funding.

Due to all the jumping through fiery hoops described in "Funny Money," I'd become myopic. My eyes were focused only on getting my basic survival needs met and I'd lost sight of the bigger physical picture—walking again. It took a friend's boxing my ears for me to appreciate that time was ticking away. There was a temporal window of spontaneous return, a healing of nerves on their own, and I was still within it. Perhaps there was a therapy out there that could unlock a cascading return of movement and sensation.

My body was crying for attention. I'd seen it go steadily downhill since my injury. For instance, a lot of my muscle tone had deteriorated from non-use. At 6'6", I was 220 pounds when I last played Frisbee. This dropped to a weight of 155 pounds. I cried when that one sank in. Muscle fiber had melted away, along with calcium from my bones. At the time, my osteoporosis equaled that of a seventy-year-old woman.

Experts agreed that spending 50 million dollars a year for spinal cord injury research could lead to a cure being found in five to seven years. Our government would be wise to fund this research, because the cost to treat and warehouse the spinal cord injured is 2 billion dollars annually!

I knew a cure for paralysis could come in as soon as five to seven years, and I needed to be ready. A daily routine of informed physical therapy and exercise was my only hope. After his injury, Christopher Reeve would spend at least eight hours a day in therapy, maintaining his muscle tone and bone density for the arrival of a medical cure.

My exercise program had been sabotaged by recurring bladder infections and mind-numbing leg and hip pain. Some days I got out of bed only to count the hours until I could go back into the sweet arms of sleep. I'd let valuable time go by and hence recommitted myself to the task of being ready for the cure.

Since Medicare and Medicaid didn't see any reason to give basic physical therapy to someone who they didn't think would ever walk again, I had to go to the private sector to raise funding for additional clinical treatment and a home exercise gym. My near future also included major expenses for dental work, physical therapy machines and a trip to the Miami Project to Cure Paralysis. None of this would be covered by either state or federal insurance, so an exercise/medical fund became my priority.

My first goal was to raise $10,000 to go to Miami, where I would finally get checked out by state-of-the-art therapists and equipment. Unlike the Petrofsky Center, which specialized in muscle stim, the Miami Project focused on various biofeedback techniques. I would also get an MRI there, to finely detail the condition of my injury site, which hadn't yet been done. Furthermore, they had specialized equipment that could precisely determine which nerves were still active and which nerves had been traumatized into inactivity. They'd also developed a surgical procedure to relieve pressure on injury sites for a dramatic increase in mobility and sensation. Although the odds were slight in my case that this could help, I had to know for sure. The trip to Miami would also get me to the people who could help get rid of the mother-of-all pains in my right leg.

I hoped to come away from the Project with an exercise regime to develop the areas highlighted as active by their biofeedback testing. My garage would have to be converted into a therapy room to accommodate a tilt table, hand crank cycle, specialized stationary bicycle and other leading edge equipment I'd been researching.

I needed a backbone of paid assistants. For me to do more than just survive the "warehouse," I had to produce $50,000 a year—an extremely ambitious goal for someone who needed help getting out of bed in the morning. But if I were to set any goal, it might as well be for what I needed to be healthy and ready for a medical cure.

If we all worked in concert together—myself, friends, family and our government—the goal of my walking down the path of life could be achieved. My days would be filled with this work. I couldn't sit back and slowly lose my potential to walk. There was more of the physical world I wanted to gobble up. I especially craved walking down a wooded path, away from the straight lines of civilization, and snorkeling in the beautiful Pacific Ocean, watching the current-driven ballet of sand pixies that first greeted me moments after my injury.

ALL THE COLORS OF THE DAY

My last chapter, "Funny Money," gave a partial story. My health went up and down—up with new sensations and down with intense pain. I was devalued from a set schedule of daily RN care to a revolving door of home health aides.

My shelter was a cramped house in a densely packed neighborhood. I shared the house with my old office partners and two caregivers, and slept in the living room (couldn't get into the tiny bedroom). In this environment, I tried to write and pull my life together. It wasn't working. I was sinking fast, but the darkest moments truly come before the dawn. Let me tell you about the sunrise that happened next and all the colors that bathed me.

THE COLORS OF CHRISTMAS

Early December: my house was cramped and filled with people, yet I felt safe in the nest of supportive friends. HUD offered to pay three quarters of my rent, but only if I lived alone in a studio apartment. Before my injury I loved living alone, but with paralysis the thought sent shock waves of fear through my body. There was just too much that could go wrong. I needed the rent support and a communal environment. I was caught in a conundrum.

After months of telephone calls and letter writing appeals to the local HUD officials, I finally proved that I was a quadriplegic in need of three live-in caregivers. HUD relented, and I was granted certification for a four-bedroom home. A wheelchair-accessible house was hunted down and leased. The Eagle had landed!

Unfortunately, most homes in Hawaii are very tiny, since land and materials for housing are so expensive. My four-bedroom home was charming, yet very small. The walls were thin, tropically designed with a single piece of wood for substance. Unless muted, conversations were involuntarily shared. The cramped hallways meant I couldn't turn into the bathroom, so I brushed my teeth in the kitchen and showered outside, which thankfully can be done year-round on Maui.

Mid-December: Christmas around the corner, and I was getting desperate. I was already down one housemate, the other evening caregiver was leaving, and for the first time since my injury, no replacement was available. I needed two people to alternate evening care and be available throughout the night. In three days' time, I would either be alone in the house some nights or risk the burnout of my one remaining caregiver—desperate straits indeed.

I suddenly remembered a friend who was traveling on the mainland. She was about to return to Maui in order to pack up her life and move. I made a phone call to her in New England and she agreed to fill in for six weeks as an evening caregiver while she prepared for the move. Great! I had a six-week reprieve, enough time to place more "Help Wanted" ads.

THE COLOR OF MONEY

Remember in the *Our Gang* series of old, when one of the gang would jump up and exclaim, "Hey! Let's put on a play!" then they all ran off and poof—it happened? A dear friend of mine had just such an inspiration one day in early July.

"Why not have a benefit for Michael's therapy fund?" he pitched. He knew four people vacationing on Maui who would make excellent speakers for a benefit lecture. He inquired and discovered that they were all willing and available, but only on one night—two weeks away! So we gathered up some friends and pulled a rabbit out of the hat.

In two weeks' time, we got press releases out, placed advertisements in papers, put up posters around the island, mailed
postcards, made announcements in churches, set up telephone trees,
broadcasted interviews and advertisements over the radio, secured a
hotel ballroom, got flowers, a sound system and stage lighting donated,
and recruited volunteers for the evening.

We filled the room with three hundred and fifty people to hear
renowned inspirational speakers Alan Cohen, Jerry Jampolsky and his
wife Diane Cirincioni, followed by Wayne Dyer and his wife! With
proceeds from the evening's gala, I was only a couple grand shy of my
Grand goal. I was definitely within spittin' distance, so I immediately
started making travel plans to Miami. By that time I'd come to believe
that my needs would always be met. I trusted that the rest of the money
would come somehow. (I could always sell a kidney.)

THE REST FROM THE MIDWEST

My family is from Omaha, Nebraska—the heartland. At the same
time we were organizing the event on Maui, my younger sister came up
with another fundraising idea: "Let's do a golf tournament!" She rallied
the family and within yet another two week time period, they pulled a
second rabbit out of the hat.

Early on a gorgeous, September Sunday morning, eighteen
foursomes hit their best wood at the sound of the shotgun (someone
was trying to shoot a birdie). Everyone began to play eighteen holes of
golf at the same time. Esoteric side games, known only to the anointed,
were enjoyed for my benefit. A luncheon with donated food and an
auction of donated items completed the day, and my trip to Miami was
assured. (Whew… close call for the kidney.)

There was one turning point without which this successful
fundraiser would only have been just another great idea. My sister
galvanized everyone into action, but one person triggered her.

Someone I'd never met encouraged her to act, even though the task
seemed too formidable. When she said, "I don't know if I can do this,"
he said, "Sure you can. I've even done the posters and some are out
already."

This man was a gentle force that moved a mountain of volunteers
into action. Initially, I wanted to know his name and thank him in
person, but then I had a second thought. I preferred him to remain
nameless so he could be everyone—the "Everyman."

We can all touch someone's life at just the right moment, in a way
that reminds them anything is possible. We can let them know they're

not alone in their struggle to achieve more or simply to survive. A timely word of encouragement costs us nothing, and can set off a positive chain reaction in someone else's life.

I believe we all have an inner knowing of what to say and do to support the other members of our communities. My Good Samaritan in Omaha is the "Everyman" in all of us.

6

GONE TO MECCA

Mecca has water?! My pilgrimage was made for physical therapy. I took a break from the fluorescent lights of a clinical, basement facility to sail under the sun in an adapted sailboat. I was at the tiller, being cautioned not to fall overboard.

FULL MOON OVER MIAMI

The time had come. The funds had been raised and I'd secured a home, so it was time to make my pilgrimage to the Miami Project to Cure Paralysis. This state-of-the-art facility was the Mecca for spinal cord injury research. Here I would finally be able to get assessed, evaluated, and begin a tailored therapy program to keep my body well maintained. Our government health programs saw me as a closed case. They had no money for therapy to maintain muscle and bone strength, integrity of joints and body alignment, all of which are needed to be able to walk. But I knew that with a cure for my injury on the near horizon, I had to be ready.

A recent émigré to Maui, a physical trainer, was a gracious volunteer who'd become a close friend. I knew he would be an invaluable asset to have at the Miami Project, so I timidly asked if he would join me. When he exploded with a vibrant "Yes, I'd be honored to come," my heart was so touched that someone would give three weeks of his life for me, I choked up.

The same thing happened when one of my caregivers volunteered to go to Miami. This was one of the core issues that my injury was forcing me to face, that I was worthy of all this love and attention. I did deserve this support. Someday soon, I hoped, it would sink in and I could check that core issue off my list.

The three of us walked down the causeway to the plane. The rigors of planning and packing had overwhelmed my thrill of traveling. I just wanted to sit and snooze while flying through the air at 400 miles an hour.

We flew in three airplanes and transferred wheelchairs nine times to get to Miami. Staying at a hotel would've been a budget buster, even if the three of us crammed into one small, cheap room. The cost of eating at restaurants would also have drained our funds. Then I discovered we could sleep under golden arches, at the Ronald McDonald House located next to the medical center in Miami.

The McDonald's Corporation has a chain of residence homes for families of children who are being treated at large children's hospitals around the country. The McDonald's refugee camps are well-appointed and primarily for these families with ill children but if there's room, other people in need can stay there.

By sleeping under their golden arches we were able to afford two rooms, and saved even more money by cooking in their large, communal kitchen. In addition, twice a week a community group would come in and fix dinner for the whole house! We felt like part of a large clan celebrating holiday feasts. Our hearts were blown open by these examples of corporate and personal compassion. (I'll never feel guilty about eating a Big Mac again.)

NON-TRANSFERABLE

The federal government, through Medicaid, had given my state, Hawaii, funding to supply me with a home health aide for three hours a day. My request to have that same service while in Miami was rejected. Suddenly, I didn't have a valid medical reason! I could only get support from my government to survive if I stayed at home like a good disabled person (forget vacations to visit family like a normal person). This basic care was imperative, so I would have to come up with the $80 per day needed to cover the cost.

My last hope was Medicare, but I had to wait until landing in Miami for an interview to find out how much help I could get. I hoped to get at least two hours a day for bathing, bowel care, exercise, dressing and getting into the chair. What I was offered was forty-five minutes! After three days of appeals, doctors' letters and phone calls, Medicare relented and provided two hours' assistance each morning.

BIOFEEDBACK LABORATORY

On November 11, our elite trio descended on the medical complex, began three weeks of tests and evaluations, picked everyone's brain and pored over the spinal cord injury reference library, sucking up like locusts everything in our path.

My daily clinical regime was to practice using exotic equipment. One such device was a computer with two processors that lived in the basement of the center. Words never appeared on the screen, just a graph with a dancing green line. The line went up and down according to the strength of a signal the computer received from electrodes connected to my muscles. The muscles were activated by stimuli that originated in my brain from the intention to move them. When asked to move my leg, the little green line didn't dance.

In between my brain and leg, at the fifth cervical joint, was where I'd gotten hurt. The injury site in my neck was like a freeway interchange in Los Angeles collapsed by an earthquake. Most of the lanes were blocked, but there was a trickle of cars that could wriggle their way through, each car being a neuron coming from the brain and aiming for a muscle. The biofeedback computer could count how many cars made it through to the muscle and displayed the count as a dancing green line on the computer screen.

Remember, after the Los Angeles earthquake, how helicopters captured video of all the traffic exploring the side streets, looking for a way to bypass the collapsed freeway? Well, that's what biofeedback training does. The screen shows you when your intention makes an alternate connection to the muscle. It may be a brief flash, but you see it and can go back again and again, thus widening the back road into a major thoroughfare.

Previously, I'd thought that I would regain use of my back and triceps muscles only if the injury site healed itself. These folks were saying that I could vastly increase the use of these muscles with intention and willpower, combined with exercise.

The first time I tried my triceps muscles they measured 5 percent of a normal signal wriggling through from my brain. After three sessions, I discovered an alternate pathway that allowed 30 percent of my intention to reach the muscle. Even a 30 percent return of my triceps could allow me to transfer myself from chair to bed and back again. Manual wheelchairs would also become feasible and further develop my upper body. The world would open up even wider with that level of added body strength.

For three weeks, I danced with that computer in the cramped basement of the biofeedback laboratory. Pushing, willing, and cajoling the green line to go up was my only goal in that darkened room.

At the end of three weeks, the head of the program summed up my biofeedback training: my shoulders and biceps were fine, most of my hands and belly were still asleep, my triceps had gone from 5 percent strength to a potential of 30 percent, my back muscles could improve to 75 percent at the top and 50 percent at the bottom, and my legs were mostly still sleeping except for that darn radiating pain.

BUSMAN'S HOLIDAY

After spending ten days within the medical center complex, we decided to go to South Miami Beach to shop and take in a movie. Not all of the city buses had wheelchair lifts, but the one to South Beach did. We traveled through some tough neighborhoods to get to the pride of Miami, the c.1920s Art Deco architectural strip facing the ocean.

After rolling and shopping for the day, we waited for a return bus in the fading afternoon light. The Saturday schedule, posted on a rusty pole, was confusing. After a thirty-minute wait, we decided to walk to another bus stop, because we couldn't afford to miss our connections back to the medical center.

Halfway to the other stop, the bus we'd been waiting for rounded the corner and zoomed past us. Our three shouting voices combined to get the driver's attention, and he quickly pulled over to the side of the road. The bus was blocking traffic, but he lowered the ramp anyway. Unfortunately, the street was severely sloped and the ramp wouldn't lie flat enough for me to get on.

Street people gathered to watch our predicament. We had to get on that bus because the sun was setting, and the street would become dangerous at night, so we'd been told. The Cuban American driver called out to my friend, "Hey! Stop traffic for me, I'm backing up to the bus stop." My friend's eyes widened with surprise, but he jumped into action, motioning traffic around a whale-sized bus reversing half a block and through an intersection.

When we arrived back at the bus stop I began struggling onto the narrow ramp. A street drunk was helping by calling out directions: "Move right, straight back, no, your wheel is off, stop!" Silently I wished him away, but the bus driver thanked him with a transfer ticket. I was humbled.

Catching this bus got us into central Miami. We knew we had plenty of time to make our connection back to the medical center, so we decided to stop at a shopping complex for dinner and a movie. It was a treat to be out past my regular 7 p.m. go-to-bed routine. Post movie, we waited at yet another bus stand and saw that the last scheduled bus on our route was due to arrive in five minutes' time, at 11:20 p.m. Good timing. It was dark, the wind was cold and I felt weary and vulnerable. The bus arrived on schedule, but after opening the doors, the driver shrugged his shoulders and said, "I'm not equipped with a ramp." Stunned, we asked what we could do.

"I dunno," he said, closing the door and driving away.

We were stuck! Couldn't call a cab; my electric wheelchair wouldn't fit in the trunk. Wheelchair taxi services didn't run that late. Other buses on different routes whisked away the remaining travelers, leaving us abandoned on the platform—a classic wheeling dilemma.

I felt I was living a scene from a movie. If so, then I wanted a happy ending. There had to be a way out. We always have options as conscious, viable, sentient beings.

"Don't worry, Michael," said a quiet voice within. "Just trust that this will all work out."

Five minutes later the same bus returned. The driver yelled out the window, "I've called the base and they're sending another bus for you." We were elated and touched that he would go off his schedule and backtrack to tell us he had called for help.

Nice guy.

Now Miami was supposed to be a dangerous city where you couldn't trust anyone on the street. Even within the medical center complex, we were warned not to go out at night. We did anyway, and often found the footsteps following us to be those of a protective security guard. Those two bus drivers showed compassion and a willingness to help. In fact, all of our encounters were heartfelt and neighborly. Miami would forever hold a warm spot in our hearts.

THE HUMAN CANNONBALL

"Yeah, let's get an MRI of your cervical area," the neurologist said. I had been suggesting it for some time, because I'd never gotten a postoperative look at my injury site. Using the pure magic of the MRI's ability to image soft tissue, I would finally know if I had either a gaping hole or viable tissue at the C 5-6 part of my spinal cord. If the cord had been too traumatized, my body would have reabsorbed the dead tissue, leaving a visible gap. If tissue had survived, it would show up. To know for sure, I had to get shoved into a cannon.

Someone somewhere had the idea to put a person inside a long, tubular magnet. Somehow a computer can read the way our bodies influence the field produced by this huge magnet, which then produces an image of soft tissue—something x-rays cannot do. It's magic, folks.

In a myriad of buildings I found the imaging center that housed two massive MRI machines. There was a waiting room for the ambulatory and an inner room for patients, who were on gurneys or in wheelchairs. Filled mostly with the elderly, this room had the somber mood of a chapel—everyone deep in thought, sharing whispers. The anxiety in the air was palpable.

Everyone had a good reason to be there, and a desire not to be. As I was lifted from chair to gurney, I tried not to think about the claustrophobic experience to come. Finally, my turn arrived to enter the shielded, metal room.

"Take off all metal—watches, jewelry and pins," the attendant advised. "The magnet will suck them right in."

I was loaded into a machine with an opening so narrow and so tight its inner ribs threatened my big nose. (Imagine the circus performer waving goodbye as he slides down the nozzle of the cannon.) Bound like a mummy and weighted down, every sort of claustrophobic image flooded back from the depths of my memory.

"OK Mr. Kanouff, we're going to start now," a metallic voice warned through the crackling speaker. I wished I'd been given a countdown to prepare me for the explosion of sound that followed. The machine surrounding me produced a droning, bass roar at the intensity of a jackhammer. For three hours I kept my eyes closed, and eventually drifted into and out of sleep. The extended stay was to image my entire spine, searching for the elusive cause of my nemesis, the fiery sciatic pain radiating down my right leg.

THE RESULTS ARE IN

The MRI film cleared my spinal disks from being the cause of my intense pain. I was told I had peripheral neuropathy in my legs, a general term that means one's nerves are screaming. In 60 percent of these cases, the white-coated people don't know why. Unfortunately, I was in this group. My last hope was that my new exercise regime would somehow correct what was wrong. Maybe since I wasn't walking, my body was just screaming at me for more movement. In any case, the renewed sensations in my lower trunk were a conduit for its flaming messages. Oh, well. Life went on.

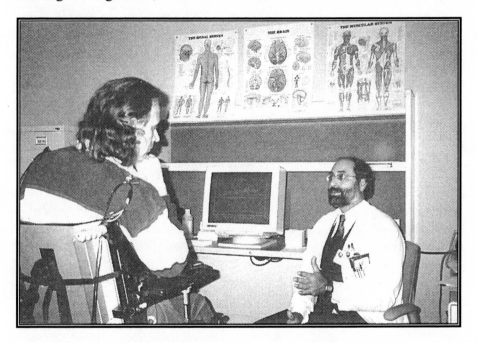

"The head of the program summed up my biofeedback training…"

The test also revealed that the hope for a miracle surgery to relieve bone pressure to the injury site was neither feasible nor necessary. And although my injury site was bruised and traumatized, there was no dreaded gaping hole. The MRI showed a clean channel for the spinal cord. It had been damaged yet there was still viable tissue. Hope springs eternal. As one Miami doctor categorically stated, "It just isn't true that you only have a one to three year window to get return sensation and motor control after your injury. You never stop healing. You can always get more return."

I have often remembered those words because hope is what carries people through life's bleakest periods. Hope is the expectation that life will renew itself. Hope is the vital element in recovering from any injury.

Why do doctors routinely keep their patients' hopes down? "Cautiously optimistic" is an apt term for what they must have been taught in medical school to curtail a patient's emotions. But this vital energy of life is what should be nourished and encouraged; not to the extreme of delusion, but to the point where a person's whole being is engaged in the healing process. At that point, something else kicks into motion.

I do feel strongly that more people would have greater return after spinal cord injuries if their medical experts said, "Go for it! We don't know the limits to these magical bodies of ours. Try everything to heal yourself, judge results by their merit, and let go of what doesn't help you. Take all the time you need, knowing that you will always get better than you are now. Don't forget to enjoy life along the path of your healing. One part of you has been injured, but still your whole being is wonderfully alive and vital. Use this to enliven others around you by your presence. Your life is richer for this experience and time will bear that out."

HOME AGAIN, HOME AGAIN, JIGGITY JIG

We concluded our grueling three weeks in Miami with another challenging up, down, up, down, up, down airplane trip, the high point of which was the first transfer in Los Angeles. While transferring me into an aisle chair to exit the plane, the airline staff let me slip through their fingers and I bounced onto the floor. This was the danger when directing inexperienced airline employees on the fine art of a chair-to-chair transfer.

Back on Maui, a small mob of friends met us at the airport and helped get me home, unpacked, massaged and put to bed. I slept for three weeks, recovering some time around New Year. With the New Year came my resolve to implement what I'd learned in Miami. I would have a therapy gym at home.

A physical therapist specializing in quadriplegia at the center had worked my limbs on the mat and complimented me on my limberness. Based on my overall good health, he outlined a regime to balance physical needs with my having a life other than therapy. Using him as a resource, I designed a personal exercise program.

The storage garage was cleaned and walled off with double doors, lights were hung and exercise equipment ordered. A hand crank cycle gave me aerobic workouts and a tilt table raised me vertically to a standing position, thus lengthening tendons, strengthening bones, toughening joints, and showing people just how tall I really am.

The crown jewel was the electrical stimulation bicycle, a reclining cycle with straps that secured my feet onto the pedals. Electrodes were stuck onto my legs and a computer fired them sequentially so my legs pedaled the bike. The benefits were more aerobics, strengthened bones, lubricated joints and increased leg muscle mass.

All spinal cord injured people were in training for the ultimate "Wheelchair Olympics." The cure was coming, but it would only be realized for those still physically able to take advantage of the reconnection. Muscle strengthening, joint lubrication and bone maintenance were some of the daily goals we set in order to be able to walk across the finish line.

If I had to pick a time to get injured, I picked the perfect era. There were so many wondrous medical devices and treatments relatively new to the scene. With the cure peeking over the horizon, I felt lucky. I knew a path to get to the prize. I just had to stay focused, slip into a daily therapy routine, maintain the inner work of self-reflection and be an asset to my loved ones and community by keeping my heart open.

HAM AND EGGS WITH A SIDE MIRACLE

I wasn't expecting miracles, but I knew that the time spent at the Miami Project would slingshot me into a higher orbit of health and happiness.

Actually, that's not true. I do expect miracles from the graceful unfolding of life. The miraculous happens all too often to be considered rare. Personally, I expect more miracles to occur when our lives and times darken with anxiety and fear. If a small balloon is squeezed in the hand, all of a sudden it pops out somewhere. If times get darker, we will see pockets of love and light popping around us to give us encouragement and fortitude.

7

DARK WATERS OF THE SOUL

"Sinking below the surface, I was in a new world! It was brighter than the darkness I'd feared. There I was, exploring that mysterious, surreal atmosphere under the waters of everyday life."

I had flown a quarter of the way around the world to go to the apex of spinal cord information and therapy. Exotic biofeedback equipment had pinpointed the alive but sleeping areas of my body. Professionals had advised me on therapy and sent me home with an equipment list. In four months, I'd had two benefits, written multiple newsletters, trained a stream of home health aides, plus planned and executed the trip to Miami. I was exhausted.

Once I caught my breath, it was time to build a therapy and office studio in the garage. Researching and ordering new and used equipment proved to be a logistical nightmare, but finally it was done. At last, I had the tools to keep my body strong and well maintained (more later about the "Boy's Own" clubhouse). But first, a few fires to put out…

My primary caregiver had given notice before I was fully rested from the Miami trip, which meant a storm of want ads, interviews and intuitive guessing were soon to follow. Even in the frenzy and fatigue, I knew I would find another caregiver, and I had friends who could help in the transition. I would survive and thrive. I knew the universe would support me; if not, I'd be toast.

WANDERING SADHU
A seeker of truth, who travels where Spirit calls

Along came an example of support out of the blue—up popped an Englishman. He was sojourning around the world exploring life and needed a place to stay while on Maui. He became a night shift person, errand runner, office worker and house cleaner. He even did windows! He was a gentle spirit who felt drawn to be in service. (He certainly helped the caregiver transition to go forward gracefully.) I tried to lure him into staying on as a caregiver, but it was his time to see the world for the first time by following the wind.

There must be a God looking over me, or at least a couple of angels or so. Just as the Englishman said goodbye, two wonderful people showed up at the door to be housemates and caregivers.

BE GONE, DULL PAIN

Years before my injury, I was driving to a photo assignment and wondered what it would be like to have chronic pain in my life. Could I will it away, meditate to disassociate, or use prescription drugs to keep the hounds from baying at the door? Seeing my freeway exit coming up, I drifted back from the daydream to the reality of driving. But eventually, that daydream became my nightmare.

Being paralyzed does *not* mean you are free from sensation in your lower body. Complete severing of the spinal cord is rare. Incomplete injury means some nerves remain connected and varying degrees of sensation can slowly return. Unfortunately, this sensory return often includes pain. Every wheeler I've asked has felt severe pain in areas below their level of injury, where they've been told they're not supposed to feel—an ironic twist for the injured.

Around two years after my injury, I began to feel a pain unlike any I ever knew existed, far surpassing what I previously thought was extreme pain (faint of heart skip this section). I lived daily with the feeling that a red hot nail was gouged and twisting into my right hip joint. The pain radiated down the underside of my leg, flared around the knee and foot, and traveled all the way down to my toes. It could also be described as sitting with a third-degree sunburn on a sandy, wooden chair for nine hours without moving. I felt trapped in an invisible cage made up of red hot ribbons of anguish.

Ordinary life stopped when the pain demanded attention. My attention span would become that of a four-year-old after a bag of Oreos. I would squirm in the chair to find a magic position. I applied ice packs and heating pads. I took Percocets. If that didn't work, I would distract myself with TV, movies, or work that didn't require concentration. Yelling into pillows sometimes helped. I tried everything to get away from my painful body.

THE CRYING GAME

On the super bad days my only relief was sitting in the middle of my studio and crying. The surrender to tears reduced my pain because I wasn't resisting or trying to escape. While melting into a puddle once, I looked up into the mirror and saw my face as that of a small child, with a quivering, down-turned mouth and raised eyebrows. For a moment I was embarrassed, but then consoled myself, "Oh well, this is what's happening. I might as well just face it."

The tears soon started to fade however, and curiously, I was disappointed. It felt so good to cry.

"Quick Michael, take advantage of the moment and think of something else to mourn."

The river flowed again. This method wasn't quite authentic, but it did wring the ol' cloth dry. And I felt better! A greater sense of being alive washed over me. The angry leg was still there, but it was more in the background of my awareness. The pain was no longer in my face, dominating my attention. There was room for other input. Pain shared the stage with other actors rather than being the sole entertainment.

This became my secret for pain control: go into the pain, surrender and fully experience it; actually locate its exact spot of origin. When I fully embraced my pain with tears, I was able to pull back from it, allowing other actors onto my life's stage.

ALL THE KING'S HORSES, ALL THE KING'S MEN

When you sit for eighteen months with varying degrees of pain, you can't help but think of ways to address it. I saw a family doctor, neurologist, chiropractors, physical therapists, nurses, Hawaiian healers, and massage therapists. I cried, tried traditional and alternative drug therapies and had an MRI of my entire spine, and yet the dance with my ghostly nemesis continued.

I didn't move my right leg for the better part of a year because it just hurt too much. Any stretching of the muscles or tendons would send me through the roof. I knew that my anguished leg would eventually shrink from prolonged contraction. The clock was ticking, so I launched stretching and exercise campaigns where I would "tough out" the pain, hoping it would be released with movement. It didn't work. The range-of-motion exercises sent my pain through the roof.

TURN THE KEY FIRST

A massage therapist and physical therapist each gave me the next pieces to the pain puzzle. One said my pain was definitely sciatic and the other relayed that this nerve comes out of the hip next to a tricky muscle, and the two of them could get into a mud wrestling contest. The muscle could tighten around the nerve, sending pain up and down my leg. Any stretching or exercise pulled on that tight muscle even more, torturing my poor sciatic nerve. To go through the door of pain relief, I had to turn the key first with massage, relaxing that particular muscle so it would loosen its grip on the sciatic nerve. Only then could I stretch and exercise the leg muscles.

Slowly, the hip muscle relented over the first two weeks of the new campaign. Slowly, the rest of the leg relaxed. Slowly, the sciatica surrendered its hold. Slowly, I took my life back. The answer was not what to do, but in what sequence to do it. So simple it had eluded all the experts. After two months the pain had gone down 70 percent and my leg once again had its full range of movement. Finally, I could sit and write for more than twenty minutes without being overwhelmed by the pain! I wasn't out of the woods yet, but at least I knew a path that led the way.

RELATIVITY

How many sane people do you know who could say, "One of my primary goals in life is to be a paraplegic?" From where I sat that was progress, a sane physical goal. Everyone knows people who are in better shape than they are, and others who are in worse shape. My pain was at the top of the charts for me and at the same time, I knew it was minimal compared to the pain of others. It was all relative, even within my own body! With time, my pain/comfort threshold had risen dramatically, and I really came to appreciate the malleability of the human condition.

As a species, we can endure living in both Arctic cold as well as tropical heat; live with any extreme for a while and it actually begins to normalize. During my season of high pain, I had a cute moment in my studio when visited by a mother, her daughter (in a wheelchair) and the daughter's friend, who was on crutches. We were all sitting in a circle when I spontaneously turned to the daughter and said, "I'd love to be a paraplegic."

She quickly turned to her friend and said, "I'd love to be on crutches."

Her friend turned to the mother and said, "I'd love to be like you."

The mother was speechless for a moment, until she turned and complimented my wonderful power wheelchair. The circle was complete.

BOY'S OWN CLUBHOUSE

It wasn't up a tree or dug into a hill, but in my garage. The glorified storage area was enclosed and became my studio/therapy room. I had a sanctuary—a place to write, think, and exercise; a room without an outside view, but made for an inner vision. The air-conditioned studio was the size of a generous prison cell, a description that one friend heard and corrected to "a monk's cell Michael, a monk's cell"—a moment of epiphany for me.

A long desk bent in the shape of an L held my computer and other office stuff. The small room also contained a standing table, a hand crank for aerobics and upper body strength, a reclining bicycle for leg muscle toning, a special machine that zapped soft tissue injuries and a noisy clothes dryer (couldn't move it).

Most of my in-the-chair hours were spent in this monastery where everything was accessible. It was a place where I could do projects, write, produce my art, and exercise my body.

MAD MAX

Three years after my injury, I finally got angry with God. People had been waiting for me to experience that dark night of the soul ever since my days in intensive care. Doctors and nurses had warned my friends and family that I was going to break down at any moment. I never did; couldn't afford that luxury when my ship was sinking and every day was spent bailing water and putting out fires.

The first years of living with paralysis were filled with nonstop activity, either to put out emergency fires or to adjust the machinery of life. I was inordinately busy following my injury, totally preoccupied with *doing*. You know the feeling. I held five benefits, moved house twice and addressed financial, bureaucratic and health issues. I'd slipped into a high adrenaline state of "fight or flight" and stayed there for three years. I was either asleep or going, going, going. I felt like a single parent with triplets. Daily life was so filled with new routines that there wasn't time to meaningfully assess my situation or to reflect on where I was going.

Those early years were like living in a cyclone, being buffeted about and thrown upside down. I craved normalcy, which was only within reach if I could get into the eye of the storm. If caregivers were consistent, my body remained healthy, money was in the bank, housing was assured, friends came every day to volunteer their help and the local video store kept giving me free rentals, only then had I been able to know the calm in the center of the paralysis cyclone. I credited my friends, who all pitched in to help salvage my ship in the stormy post spinal cord injury seas, with keeping me afloat.

Finally, the storms abated. There was more time in the day to relax and explore my new life—alone. I was sinking deeper into the reflecting pond called Myself. My view was of a little boy eager to learn new things. I also saw a man forty-four years old trying to stay afloat and make the best out of the situation at hand, and an old man deeply tired and afraid of dying alone. If I could be all three of these characters, then there must be a fourth, the Watcher. From his viewpoint, everything was on track except for one thing; I couldn't move much of my body.

I began to remember and miss tight-roping a curbstone for blocks on end until my feet could navigate on their own, lifting and straining to empty a truck full of photographic equipment and driving a car mapless through country familiar only by its sky. And I missed traveling alone and spontaneously as an adventurer, not an accompanied medical patient.

"It's not fair!" I screamed inside for the umpteenth time. "I should be able to move freely about this world without planning for months in advance!"

That scream echoed again in my mind as a friend described his upcoming trip to California for the holidays.

"My son and I are going to spend Saturday hiking across Golden Gate Park, then we will see a couple of movies…"

As he droned on, my heart dropped but I kept a frozen smile on my face and murmured, "Oh, that will be great. Sounds like a winner. All that in six days?"

Although I felt depressed and quietly angry, I didn't need to show him my pain. He was just being… normal.

"God damn it, why am I having to live this way?" I said out loud after he left. "It's just not fair!"

Up to that point, daily life following my injury had been dealing with one fire after another—and I was deeply tired. Those fires were truly emergency survival situations that I focused my whole being on extinguishing. The shortlist was: move into and adapt a house, secure a van, find caregivers, petition the state for an electric chair that fit my frame, research how to get useful drugs that were only available overseas, find another house, get another van, interview yet more caregivers, produce five benefits, travel twice to the mainland for therapy, fight ubiquitous bladder infections, battle dramatic cutbacks in healthcare funding, find yet another house that HUD would approve, train yet more caregivers (forty-five up to that point), and research and purchase therapy equipment. (It was important to stay active, I guess.)

DEEPER REFLECTIONS ON DEEP WATERS

Following that initial period of blazing activity, my life's stormy waters eventually quieted. I finally had more free time to look beyond the surface reflection of appearances and gaze more deeply into my new life. What I saw scared me to the core. I tried to avoid it; even fabricated heroic things to do to avoid the calm stillness inside of me where it stood. I denied embracing it in its entirety, but finally it broke through. "I'm paralyzed! (Who said that?)"

My broken body seemed to me only a fraction of its former self. "Nope, don't want to see that! I will stay busy and distracted," was my mantra. By avoiding embracing my paralysis, I remained broken in two. My lower body was floating in the waters of immobility. My upper body was doing its best to hold itself upright in the walking world (I was just shorter, that's all). But my arms couldn't pull me up and out, and I was tired of treading water. Those months were the dark night of my soul. It was time to relax, surrender to the deep, enfolding waters of the inevitable, and embrace my new life in its entirety.

Sinking below the surface, I was in a new world! It was brighter than the darkness I'd feared. There I was, exploring that mysterious, surreal atmosphere under the waters of everyday life. My first report: I wasn't alone under the water. Other people were down there, too.

When I was first injured, I knew deep down my experience had to be relevant to others, even those without my particular injury, and that I had to share it. We're all in a time of great transition on this planet. Everyone has challenging moments and much religious and philosophical literature describes going through the darkness and the fire as an essential process for the soul's refinement, only thank God we don't all do it at the same time!

So if you notice a friend or family member wrestling with themselves or with the angels, reach out a loving hand of support. Let them know they're not alone in their painful process of transition. Whisper in their ear, "Courage. Hold on. Something wonderful is ahead."

8

HALF EMPTY, HALF FULL

No legs (on the table)! Previous worktables had confining legs that I kept knocking into and breaking with my wheelchair. In my new studio, I decided to float an L-shaped plywood tabletop from the ceiling with long metal rods (a single one is seen in the foreground). I could move around all sides without fear of bruising my toes.

During my first post-injury encounter with a person in a wheelchair, a tiny part of me turned away. As I adjusted to my new world, others in wheelchairs continued to cross my horizon. We had met soon after my injury, at benefits and meetings, but my eyes had been closed to their lives for two reasons: I was too preoccupied stabilizing my life physically and emotionally, and wheelchairs scared me. Talk about not being politically correct! Even being in a wheelchair myself, I could see the vestiges of a prejudicial reaction to others in wheelchairs!

Walkers instinctively turn away from wheelers at first sight—if not physically, then emotionally. It must be that the sight of a wheelchair partially equates to death and pain. Times changed, however, and many people began to turn their attention back rather quickly to say "Hello!"

Of course there were the perpetually not smart people, too. At a Christmas party one year, I was speaking with the female half of a couple and she gave the following account: "It was really nice meeting you. I wanted to introduce you to my boyfriend, but he didn't want to come too close. He said, 'I don't want to get near that guy. He must have really heavy Karma.'"

I was never told quadriplegia was an infectious disease.

Overcoming my own prejudice, I finally began "seeing" others in wheelchairs and took the opportunity to schmooze. My initial nervous anxieties melted with each conversation. I became transfixed with every nuance of their lives—how they did this, problem solved that, danced with the ever present bureaucracies and prejudices, etc. They were so inspiring I began to see them as role models. In fact, all the people I've met who have endured a spinal cord injury have this in common: they are sincere, realistic, and have huge hearts. Something about having your ego shattered through a death and rebirth lifts the veil of personal illusion.

FREEDOM TO ROAM

The senior Bush administration did a very good thing. It passed the Americans with Disabilities Act, giving the disabled an open invitation to roam our streets and public buildings. Before this legislation I imagined only valiant paraplegics venturing out, with wheelchairs that could magically pop up curbs or even go down stairs! (Paraplegics can drive any car they can lift themselves into, with hand controls installed.) Quadriplegics really liked a flat surface and the occasional chairlift. Many either had their own vans with lifts and hand controls, or just stayed home in their immediate neighborhoods.

The ADA cost a lot of people a lot of money to ramp, elevate, cut, widen, and sociologically modernize the architectural and transportation systems of America. I think we were worth it. When I took an accessible bus it felt like I was on my own private $200,000 stretch limo (but who were all those other people at the wet bar?).

Even though all public spaces were supposed to be accessible, I did run into a few that were so in name only—but only a few. Mostly, the world was wide open to wheelers, and they began showing up everywhere.

One of my favorite examples of an uninhibited spirit is John Hockenberry, a radio journalist for *NPR* and then correspondent for *ABC News*. He's also a paraplegic who could climb curbs. He's been everywhere. My favorite story in his autobiography *Moving Violations* is his account of flying into Tehran and covering the Ayatollah Khomeini's funeral. Upon arrival, he rented a driver and his pickup truck and bounced into the dusty countryside, surrounded by over a million mourners on foot. A constant crush of people swarmed around the casket, which was being carried on the arms of whoever could fight their way to these esteemed positions. He set his chair on the gravel road and courageously plunged into the sea of mourners. He got close enough to see the Ayatollah's casket slip to the ground, where it broke into pieces, exposing the body. (Too many cooks...) Hockenberry gives a vivid description of the enshrouded body being hoisted upon the hands of the multitudes and trundled down the road.

There are stars in the galaxy of the paralyzed and then there are the people in our neighborhoods, equally brilliant, equally facing challenges and coming up with creative solutions. Some are in their third decade, others haven't rolled a year yet. In any case, having a spinal cord injury tests your mettle and deepens your resolve. Knowing we were on a similar road, a journey of transformation, deepened my respect for other wheelers that I met.

QUADRIPLEGIC HEROES ON MAUI

P. married his nurse, combined two families, and restarted his electrical contracting company. Every weekday at 3 p.m. he would delicately maneuver his wheelchair van through a school parking lot full of children, looking for his own.

K. brought three Buddha babies into this world after her injury! I knew anything was possible when I heard her description of changing babies' diapers without fingers that grasp. As her children grew older, she decided it was "time to go back to school."

One has to put pressure on bones to keep them strong.
I used a tilt table to keep up my bone mass and show off my height.

J. lived alone, drove her own car, and swam every day in the ocean. Her rehab graduation exercise was to show that she could get from her wheelchair to the floor and back again without any assistance. J. was ecstatic about her artwork in clay and the support of God's love in her life. She met a beloved at church and they lived happily ever after.

D. migrated from San Diego to a beachside home on Maui's northern shore. Using a hand splint he became a noted painter in oils, although he eventually bought a laptop, so it was goodbye to oils and hello to computer illustration programs.

H. was a role model because nothing could ever stop her from being socially active. Wherever two or more were gathered the third was H. Workshops, benefit dances, campouts, hikes, parties and political hearings all had the presence of her smiling, beneficent countenance. She was a tireless political activist, exploding like a skyrocket into space as a champion for the physically challenged.

With a computer for mission control, her thoughts were manifested through a box that listened to her voice and did her bidding. No more waiting for a friend to type a letter, and with the Internet no more waiting for someone to take her to the library for research. The Internet became more to her than a word from the lexicon of a technological high priesthood. It became her avenue to stroll at will.

Computers have opened the world to the physically challenged. This is an electronic, barrier-free world, with an unthinkably vast library of instant information and communication. This world is new for all of us, and I predict the giants of this emerging culture will be the people we once considered handicapped.

UNNATURAL CYCLES

"Oh please work, oh please work," I muttered under my breath. I was at the computer loading my new voice recognition software, a program that allowed me to write quickly using my voice. I would've been a slow hunt and pecker without it.

Much of my new life was spent writing. It was meaningful work to me and besides, everyone seemed equal on a computer, although I soon encountered a frustrating problem that made me feel handicapped with this technological marvel.

When the air conditioner came on in my studio, it made so much noise the computer microphone couldn't hear me clearly. Bizarre words would appear on the screen and I had to go back and fix them manually.

At first this was such a large problem my initial enthusiasm for writing waned. Even a short note could become so frustrating I'd end up smashing the computer.

WACKPHHSSS!!!! The monitor made the loudest noise as it was bashed. WHAMWHAMWHAM!!!! The computer box itself took a number of blows before it was unrecognizable. HHHHSSSSSSS!!!! Smoke from the sparking wires made me cough, but it was worth it; the intense frustration was relieved.

This was all in my head, of course. I only had the option of a few physical release techniques, so I'd refined my 3-D, Technicolor, mental movie sets to deal with my frustration.

Eventually, I accepted what I couldn't change and went on with the flow of life. When the air conditioner cycled off, I would jump in and start writing. After the room warmed up and the air conditioner came back on, I made my daily phone calls. When the pervasive rumbling stopped, the quiet stillness would again be the starting gun to write as much as I could.

I eventually bought the newer version of the voice recognition program, hoping it would be better, but there was no improvement. Alas, the air conditioner won. I surrendered. Fortunately, winter was coming. Unfortunately, winter only lasts two months on Maui. Fortunately, an unlimited number of virtual computers existed for me to fantasy-bash. Unfortunately, this gave me headaches. Fortunately, I moved to a cooler region of Maui, where I didn't need an air conditioner—just the tradewinds. Also fortunately, voice recognition programs evolved to a higher state.

THE NEXT STEP

The research on repairing damage to the spinal cord was maturing, with human trials on the horizon. One simple experiment: just fill in any gaps in the cord from a spinal injury with an injection of living cells. The immediate goal was not to re-enervate for movement or sensation, but simply to have the injected cells survive. "Patching a pothole" with living tissue was a necessary first step for subsequent road repair.

In another line of research, scientists went up the nose of an artificially paralyzed rat and took a scraping of the nerve endings that sense odor. These "olfactory ensheathing cells" have a particular quality of growing like bamboo during the rainy season. The specialized cells know how to communicate with their neighbors and grow long tendrils up into the brain. Somehow researchers got these cells to multiply in a petri dish, injected them into the rat's spinal lesion, and the little guy eventually started to tap dance (I didn't know if this was for me. I'm more of a free form jazz dancer).

Gadget packs of researchers were also having fun with implanted electronic devices. One approved procedure was to implant electrodes into arm muscles. A power switch and supply source would be hidden in the chest. A person could reach out for the telephone with one hand (most quadriplegics can move their arms and wrists), thump their chest with the other hand, and the electrodes would trigger the muscles that close the fingers. Chat away.

These examples are just a tiny sampling of the many news items that crossed my desk. Scientific breakthroughs were traveling at near light speed. Some stories almost instantly became ancient history. There were many avenues of research, but the most promising of all, and the eventual therapy of choice, would almost certainly be based on stem cells.

9

TIME AFTER TIME

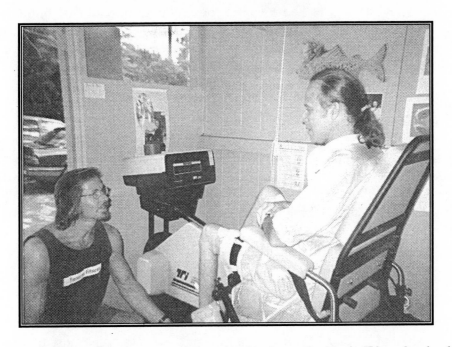

The crown jewel of my therapy equipment was this electro-stim bicycle. Electrodes placed on my legs were fired sequentially so that my own muscles pedaled the bike. This routine helped retain muscle mass and bone density and increased circulation; "a day in the life" wouldn't be complete without it.

I'd been exploring my Brave New World for four and a half years. Every day was unique—learning new skills, facing extreme challenges, and overcoming personal fears that shook the very foundation of who I thought I was. The great and the miraculous also occurred, but at times it seemed I was taking one step forward and three back. "Perseverance Furthers," says the *I Ching*.

Much of my daily routine revolved around pain management. In addition to sciatica, incessant bladder infections left me loopy from pain and the requisite medications. The drugs did give me some pain relief, but also wandering attention, poor short-term memory and debilitatingly low blood pressure. The nearly constant infections left me with the impression that feeling bad was normal. Some days I got up only to count the hours until I could return to bed and the sweet relief of sleep.

During this time of battling infection, another physical infirmity literally darkened my horizon. Perfect vision had always been my ally. Whenever I read, watched a sunset, or explored the universe through my camera or computer, my eyesight extended my body's reach.

When my ability to close focus degenerated, I got fitted for reading glasses. I shrugged, "Oh well, it's that forties thing." Then, on the fourth anniversary of my injury, I cried "Not me!" A blood clot, a danger common to the paralyzed, had lodged in my retina and I lost vision in the center of my left eye.

These and many other traumatic speed bumps forced me to raise the white flag. I gave up trying to accomplish external goals. Forget socializing; I couldn't even complete sentences without crying. Without being engaged in outside activities, I was forced to be with myself. I felt a deep stirring there inside of me, a quickening of the soul. The hint of something profound, shimmering in my peripheral vision, excited me.

Time after time throughout my whole life, I felt something trying to meet me halfway. It was subtle, always in my periphery, and yet eager to lend a hand, encouraging me to take the next step.

ANOTHER DAY IN THE LIFE

The day-to-day life of a quadriplegic isn't a routine most people would normally know. To an outsider it might seem surreal. I promised myself early on to be very candid in unveiling my life as a spinal cord injured person, hoping that a deeper understanding of my experience would engender compassion for all disabled people. So here's another travelogue of the world I walked, a few years later than my first. It's both different and the same.

The morning chill pulled me out of a dream into the waking world. I hid behind closed eyelids. Even though I was shivering I kept my eyes closed, trying not to move my body or the covers any more than I had to. I took only shallow breaths. My body wanted to stretch and spasm, but I couldn't let it. Any movement, even a deep breath, would trigger an earthquake swarm of muscle contractions that could leave me in pain for the rest of the day.

"Don't move, Michael, don't move," was my mantra.

I knew by the increasing light in the room that the morning aide wouldn't be in for another hour. "Don't move."

I'd been lying on my back for twelve hours. My whole body was poised to spasm. The good thing about these involuntary movements was that my muscles got exercised and toned by their isometric tug on my skeletal frame. The bad thing about these muscle contractions was their strength. Those that were tied down to my lower spine could even pull the vertebrae out of alignment. Then the poor ol' nerves coming out of the spinal column would get squished as they peeked their heads out. One large spasm and those nerves could radiate exquisite pain down my leg for the next eighteen hours. No fun.

The state-supplied home health aide would walk through the door at 7 a.m. For the next three hours I did my well-choreographed routine. My legs got the first dance with range of motion, stretching exercises. They were slowly moved in a specific sequence while they jerked and tugged with smaller, safe spasms.

Hawaiian homes tend to be tiny; narrow hallways and small bathrooms meant I either had a bed bath or showered outside. Unless it was really stormy, I preferred the outdoor shower. I would be loaded into a waterproof wheelchair, rolled out the front door and locked into place halfway down the driveway. A hot water hose was threaded through the kitchen window. The hot, running water felt great. I was quite a sight to behold, sitting there steaming on cold winter mornings. No one ever saw me though, except for the startled UPS driver delivering his packages.

If it was a bowel day, then I'd go boweling. What went in had to come out. Urinary tract and anal sphincters wait patiently for signals from the brain to relax and open up, but for the paralyzed those signals don't make it through. Death would've been on the horizon if it weren't for the built-in wisdom of the body. A suppository would trigger the chain of events needed to defecate. Then I sat up in one of those "potty chairs" or rolled over onto my side and used a bedside commode.

Imagine my surprise the first time I emptied my bowels this way in the hospital. My ego was completely deflated when the nurse had to include a digital stimulation to get things moving. Now digital in that case meant finger and stimulation meant a deep sense of letting go.

The next time you watch *ER* or another emergency room medical show, listen to what they usually say at the very beginning of a patient's arrival: "Get a Foley in him." Newly injured people still gotta pee. A Foley is a catheter that snakes its way up the penis and through the sphincter into the bladder. A small balloon at the tip inflates to the size of a nickel. This anchors the catheter inside the bladder, allowing urine to constantly drain.

Immediately following my injury, I had one of these catheters put in. It drained into a bag camouflaged on the back of my chair. The system worked, except the implanted catheter was a highway for bacteria to get into my bladder. Subsequent bladder infections became my nemesis. I tried every remedy, including antibiotics (how in the world did we ever survive infection without them?). Ultimately however, the effectiveness of my efforts was limited. But there was another way…

The catheter in my penis was an implanted foreign object, a constant source of infection. I chose a different option. A surgeon cut a small hole below my belly button through to the bladder. This small opening held only the inflated catheter tip and so was less of an irritant to my body. Because it was also easier to keep clean, the "suprapubic" catheter overall presented less threat of infection to my bladder. The catheter was connected to a drainage bag, which was emptied before I got dressed.

After being dressed in bed, I had my legs swung over the side of the bed and would be lifted up to a sitting position by my arms. A small sliding board was tucked underneath me, bridging across to the seat of the wheelchair parked alongside. With a lift and a wiggle, I would slide onto the chair. I was vertical again!

After setting me up with a breakfast tray and medications for the day the aide would be gone, usually by 10 am. I didn't have the resources to hire people to work with me during the day, although I did have housemates who traded their rooms for evening care. My goal was to be self-sufficient from 10 a.m. to 6 p.m.

Maui is too small for a bus system and too rural to have sidewalks. Without any public transportation, I practiced being Monk Michael. I did get away from my studio on days when a friend would volunteer to come over for a three-hour shift. I had huge lists of things to do that required fingers. But on volunteer-free days, I had to fend for myself.

Everyone every day answers to the other call of nature—eating. There was something about having food for a goal that made me get very creative and determined.

CHIPS AHOY

The kitchen was small but I could get to a table that held a microwave and a bookstand. Most mornings I was set up with a bowl of fresh salad on the table. On top of the salad was a frozen TV dinner tray. Not a real one, but a segmented Tupperware tray filled with a frozen homemade lunch. A towel was thrown over the stack to hold the cold until mid afternoon. So the frozen dish kept the salad cool until it was time for lunch. I rolled in at lunchtime, wrestled the defrosted TV dinner into the micro and began eating the salad and reading my book.

I used my eyes to read the book and took advantage of my right hand's natural curve to hold the fork. In the whole kitchen, there was only one fork for Michael. Everyone recognized it and no one used it because of its huge, two-inch-thick black handle. I'd found the fork and its companion spoon while thumbing through a disability catalog one day.

"Corn chips would be great with this lunch," I thought, but they were in the larder. My attention completely shifted to getting that bag of corn chips out of the tiny closet. With my fork I pried open the door, strategically parking my chair underneath the shelf and reaching up to nudge the bag into a free fall. As the bag tumbled down, I batted it with my arms. In that half a second, I aimed the chips to land in my lap. They were mine!

Then I moved on to opening the bag. Couldn't tear it with my teeth. My fingers didn't pull. A bear hug wouldn't pop it. Sigh... so close and yet so far. "Put it aside Michael, don't slip into reckless frustration," I cautioned myself.

I ate more of my salad and continued craving the corn chips, still sitting there, staring up at me. One more bear hug; still didn't work. More salad, a little book reading and then the idea, "I'll stab it!"

"Concentrate, Michael. The bag will roll off to the side if you don't stab it exactly in the middle," buzzed my brain. I had a ballpoint pen in my mouth, clamped down with my back teeth. I was making blue trails all over the bag until at last I hit it directly in the center. "Pop, shewizzzz!" Then I had to gut it up the middle and jostle chips onto my plate of salad. Hooray! Another skill went into my tool bag.

When you lose some of your sensing ability, the part that remains can become quite hypersensitive. For instance, the sense of taste can become exalted, with taste buds growing to sequoia proportions. But overeating can have serious side effects—getting fat, having a Buddha belly, love handles for ten, being chunky all over, becoming "Mr. Michelin Man" or having children call out "Hey Mommy! There goes a cement truck."

Food tastes so great it's hard not to have it become an obsession, but there's no way to exercise away the calories of a typical American diet. If you're in a wheelchair, the skin of your buttocks can die of blood starvation because of the intense weight from above. Home health aides will become even harder to find if you become too mountainous to move.

For me personally, I found a middle way. My working hours were cut in half by my injury. On average, I had only eight hours of activity and free time a day. I resented spending one-fourth of it eating, so I focused on healthy, quick food with plenty of nutritional supplements and assumed permission from God to eat all the red meat I wanted in an effort to replace some of the 50 pounds of muscle that had melted away after my injury. I drew the line at liver, though. (What do people see in this stuff that ends up in hot dogs?)

THE CHILD'S WAY

Following my injury, I practiced and acquired a new skill—the practice of rapt attention. When I moved physical objects in my environment I had to be 110 percent present and attentive, since my fingers didn't grasp and only half my arm muscles responded.

My right hand had about a five percent ability to pick up a very light object. If I reached out to pick up a vitamin bottle, my whole awareness had to stay focused on my hand. I watched it and cheered myself on, "Hold on Michael, you can do it." If I let my attention wander slightly, the object would plummet to the floor.

Many days were filled with little problem-solving projects like the corn chips. Intense focus became my practical exercise of meditation: holding one thought. It was actually fun, and I was reminded of being a kid again, when there wasn't anything looming over me bigger than figuring out how to get the bicycle chain back onto the gears.

CINDERFELLA

Volunteers would often come over mid-afternoons to help around the house or take me into town to run errands and catch movies. I was driven to one summer movie in shorts and short sleeves. The air conditioner wasn't working in the van, so I used a water bottle to spray my skin for cooling. Since theaters are notoriously cold and I had a semi-reptilian nature (very little shivers or sweats), I pulled on long pants and a sweatshirt in the parking lot. I also brought along two small woolen blankets. Once inside, I bundled up and sat at the back of the bus to watch the film, errr... I mean I sat in the wheelchair area at the rear of the theater. I was quite a sight when I rolled back out into Maui's 85-degree weather. The line of tourists waiting for the next show saw me and ran back to their cars for sweaters.

"I have to get back home," I thought, as I emerged from the afternoon movie. Other friends were going to dinner. I passed. My carriage turned into a pumpkin at 6 p.m. A housemate would be fixing dinner then and at 7 p.m. would help me into bed for my two-hour nightly routine of exercise, massage, medications, pillowing and environmental adjustments.

By 9 p.m., I was precisely positioned in bed with twelve bolstering pillows, to sleep all night on my back. Lights out at 10 p.m. Alone again. Lights on at 3 a.m. The intercom buzz probably produced a groan from the housemate/caregiver on call—time for another round of medications, discharging muscle tension in my legs, adjusting blankets, and draining two thousand CCs of urine from my catheter bag.

"Quick, fall back to sleep. Stop thinking," I groggily intoned.

In three and a half hours the morning aide would be walking through the bedroom door. Even then, some bird was calling the sun.

I'M MELTING

When I lost the ability to move much of my body, I went into a free fall with my ego kicking and screaming. Different foundations of my life had crumbled into sand, and much of what I thought made up Michael Kanouff wasn't there anymore.

Being paralyzed stopped more than my muscles. Who and what I thought I was, the mental picture of myself, slowly died, went away, bye-bye. Like an onion, I saw there were layers underneath layers of self-identity that had built up since childhood. Normally these layers get peeled away gradually from mid-life onward to old age. Those with a major life crisis get to do many layers in a painfully short time.

The similarity between what I was facing and actual death was profound. My ego, part of my self-identity, was in the final stages of dying. Elisabeth Kübler-Ross's writings on death and dying are essential for anyone training to be a hospice worker or who is or has a loved one in the last phases of life. Actually, we all face death, and it takes a lot of courage to approach this subject openly. This author does so, eloquently presenting various phases of grieving and dying.

Kübler-Ross denotes the stages as Denial, Anger, Bargaining, Depression and Acceptance (DABDA). They must sound familiar to those who've gone through a major crisis. For several years after my injury, I found myself working on the last two. Depression was a traveler who dropped often into my roadhouse. His stays were both long and short. He went on his way when I mourned and accepted that another little piece of my ego identity was turning to dust.

Good! This dusting was ultimately good for me. What lie underneath when I shed a layer of my personality was the real prize, anyway. (The word personality is from the Greek *persona*, meaning "mask." What was it covering?) I was getting glimmers of my core out of the corners of my eyes. I could see that I was meant to be more than a contented "happy camper" in a wheelchair, glad to be alive with just food and a television.

There is something deeper in all of us waiting patiently to be discovered, waiting for the din of everyday life to be quieted down. For me, this homecoming was meeting a new acquaintance as well as an old friend. Each tragedy, every life crisis, or simply an upheaval of the norm presented an opportunity to excavate and know this deeper part of myself. This journey was not a comfortable one at first, but turned out to be a valid avenue in the returning "Home" process that is a major tenet of every religion.

Five years into my injury, I finally started to feel more at home. I was appreciative of what I had and not bent out of shape over what I didn't have. My friendships were richer and my ability to give and receive love had deepened. When I really went on to the happy hunting ground, I trusted that the life that flashed before my eyes wouldn't merely be filled with how much money I made or my position in society, but with the wonderful relationships I had and how much love I'd given and received.

I felt more alive because of my little deaths.

SECTION II

THE BIG IDEAS

If wisdom, born of experience, can be passed down through the ages, then the younger generations don't have to reinvent the wheel. I've had a lot of time to think about everything surrounding my injury, and I hope my Big Ideas ring true and are of some help to everyone reading this book.

10

A STEP BEYOND

"A common denominator of all my life experiences has been that no matter how dire the circumstances seemed, I could always take another step."

In talking with other wheelers, I discovered a consensus that on average, it takes five to seven years after a spinal cord injury to normalize into a new life. The early years, filled with medical fluctuations, financial traumas and emotional storms, finally give way to stability. Then the real work of building a bedrock foundation for personal growth can begin. Granted, everyone is unique and my survey was unscientific, but I offer this rough timeline to give hope that there's light at the end of the tunnel for those just beginning the arduous task of creating a new life.

After five years of hard work learning to live with paralysis, I finally began to relax. Without the distraction of putting out all sorts of fires, I got a glimpse of the gears and levers that drove my personality. By looking at what was behind the curtain, I broke the mesmerizing trance of the great "Oz." It was a fleeting moment, but finally, after twenty-five years of poking around self-help groups and considerable self-reflection, I began to see the deep, underlying mechanics that had driven me since my youth.

Without my spinal cord injury I probably would've missed this golden ring on the merry-go-round, because of the frenzy of ordinary life. Of course part of me would rather not have been paralyzed and so stayed hypnotized, but the inherent beauty of deep self-discovery was very alluring and my obvious path.

WORKING MOMS

After my injury, I was dropped into the world of professional caregivers. Dozens of them rotated through my home, so I became an astute student of home health care.

Caregiving was one of the fastest growing occupations in the U.S., and home health personnel agencies were always on the lookout for good employees. Baby boomers' parents were hiring caregivers to assist them with the tasks of daily living so they could continue to live at home. If they had medical needs, a visiting nurse would knock at their door.

In fact, an unnamed source (my eldest sister) heard at a nursing conference that the future of hospitals would be to house only those patients needing critical care. Everyone else would be treated at home, connected to hospitals by electronic monitoring systems and occasional visits from a medical professional.

With rising healthcare costs, declining budgets and families in crisis, the need for us to take care of each other is great. On the east coast of America, one test program for community care has already proved its value. It is hugely successful and wildly expanding, foreshadowing things to come.

The recently retired, with time on their hands, would visit the homes of elderly people who needed assistance in order to stay in their homes. Shopping, cleaning, meal preparation and most importantly companionship were given—not for money, but for credits. When the recently retired themselves grew older and needed help, their accounts were utilized and drawn down to get daily assistance from the next generation of the newly retired. Very clever. Very tribal.

Why are the people entrusted to care for our children as daycare workers or our parents and the disabled as home health aides paid so little? Healthcare agencies have their hands tied by the shrinking of funds from insurance companies and state and federal governments. Each year there is more to do with less. Since there's a low ceiling for pay increases, many do not make home healthcare a career; turnover is high and budget constraints don't allow for any overlapping training time. The quality of care goes down and patients suffer, which only makes the system more expensive to maintain. Everyone loses.

In my experience, aides were paid a little bit more than minimum wage. Many were single mothers working paycheck to paycheck while scrambling for time to spend with their children. Their caregiving shifts were patchworked throughout the day, often at irregular hours. Many were not paid for travel time or car mileage. Often their hours were kept at just under full-time, which made them "independent contractors," not covered by health insurance. But I did see some change coming.

The government having reverence for those in need is the glue of an honorable civilization. As a society, we are waking up to the core need of nurturing our children and honoring our elders and the disabled. The next step will be the valuing of those people who care for our children, elderly and disabled with more pay and a greater stature in society. Professional caregiving will be considered an esteemed career choice, like teaching or nursing.

France has taken this step for its young. Daycare is provided for working parents free of charge. Daycare workers have an esprit de corps attitude, because the French government takes them seriously, realizing that quality daycare helps produce civilized citizens. They've seen that it's cheaper in the long run to nurture children to be their best than to install metal detectors in schools. (Though it still doesn't explain why they like Jerry Lewis so much.)

SHOCK THERAPY

For the first several years after my injury, I'd been completely engaged in the building of a new life. Every day there was a new challenge to address, which really kept me on my toes. I was always on guard. With the eventual luxury of relaxing into a routine lifestyle came the vivid understanding that I'd had a pressure slowly building up inside of me.

Tension slowly builds up in our lives like magma increasing in pressure under a volcanic dome. Before an eruption, emotional lava oozes out of the side vents onto our family and friends. Not fair.

I was snapping at people at inappropriate times, getting very angry over little things, and frozen with apathy when large problems arose. I was easily startled, and had a short attention span, deep feelings of being overwhelmed, fears of trying something new, periodic depression, and this foolish vision of the 49ers getting to the Super Bowl. I was suffering from the accelerating symptoms of unresolved trauma, also known as toxic stress.

My symptoms were textbook signs of unresolved stress from traumas big and small. My doctor said, "Try Prozac."

My counselor said, "Try completing the cycle of traumatic stress." I might've gone looking for an accessible cliff if not for my counselor and a book he recommended, *Waking the Tiger*, by Peter Levine.

Levine wonders why some animals in the wild don't seem to suffer from stress. A gazelle, for instance, can have a life or death experience every day and still not chew its fingernails. Why?

Here's the picture: the tiger chases the gazelle. They both run at top speed, adrenaline squirting all over the place. When the tiger grabs its throat, the gazelle can no longer do "fight or flight," so it does what many mammals do to survive—it goes into shock and plays dead. The gazelle also doesn't want to be around when the tiger starts tearing it apart.

Curiously, the gazelle's going into shock and leaving its body is also a strategic move. There's a chance the tiger will drag its catch, limp and lifeless, off to a tall tree. When the tiger looks up to see which branch would make a nice picnic table, it releases its prey from the death grip. The gazelle, flickering in and out of consciousness, sees an opportunity and Zooom!! The tuckered tiger looks down and looks out to see the gazelle already out of reach.

Once it's safely at a distance, the gazelle throws off the effects of its life or death trauma—it begins to shake and convulse. It may even keel over, feet in the air, trembling uncontrollably from the internal earthquake. After a moment the shaking stops and the gazelle is back on its feet, grazing as if nothing had happened!

Levine notes that animals in the wild go through a full cycle of physiological release after being in crisis. If the cycle is successfully completed, the body not only physically "shakes out" the adrenaline, but the fear and tension as well. All mammals naturally complete this cycle, except for you know who. We humans tend to choke off our emotions and tighten our bodies in a constant state of "fight or flight." Even guards protecting a military perimeter need to take breaks and relax in a safe place to let off steam.

My safe shelter was expressing my emotions. Instead of shaking to release the impact of my injury, I cried. For years I would cry at the drop of a hat, tearing at something as simple as a pair of eyes expressing a soul. When I physically beat and screamed into a few pillows, I found an even deeper sense of peace.

We all have places in our personalities protected by "Do Not Enter" signs—and that's okay. It's a valid way to keep painful experiences from overwhelming us. Unfortunately, it does reduce the scope of our lives.

I found myself digging into the layers of stress and trauma I had buried throughout my whole life. Guess what? A treasure was hidden down there. The catch? It was guarded by a fearful monster—my having to consciously re-experience the original pain and complete the cycle.

If anything even looked similar to a buried painful experience, it would trigger an unconscious avoidance and denial, or a "playing dead" to the ghostly grip of the tiger. If I was not able to respond consciously, then oops... there was a disability. By keeping my eyes open and facing into the shock waves of past trauma that were still echoing in my psyche, I could reopen territories I'd long ago fenced off.

I was extremely excited about peeling back the subtle layers that had protected me throughout the years, which promised a richer quality of life than ever before. It was like digging sharp rocks out of a garden so my life could grow even more lush and abundant.

Years on, I figured I would probably be embarrassed at my standing on a soapbox about this internal understanding, but at least for a time it seemed to be my "job."

A common denominator of all my life experiences has been that no matter how dire the circumstances seemed, I could always take another step. Even if it seemed like I was stepping off into an unknown void, my feet always landed on something firm that supported my life.

Einstein mused, "The ultimate question is whether the universe is friendly." With every step, I've found that it is just that.

11

LIFE SUPPORT

In our early years, we can be confident of support and protection from our parents. As adults we can stand independently, but we're also interdependent; we all need some help.

Most people don't know about a certain aspect of quadriplegia. After a year of this new life, aliens take over our bodies for arcane medical research. They start by inducing arching, full body spasms. Oh, that was an episode of *X-Files*. Uh… I'll start over.

Within a year of their new lives, most quadriplegics have to start a boarding house. Not all; some can go back to live with their blood families, who become their primary caregivers. Others receive large insurance settlements and can hire all the help they need. Some have to live in nursing homes because they're destitute and alone, but most get a big house where they can trade rooms to people for daily care.

I was able to get a big house, with housemates as caregivers. I would advertise, sometimes for months, for good people who could work evenings and be on call a couple of overnights a week. They would cook dinner and help me with exercise, medications, and getting to bed at night. I had to make good hiring decisions because I spent so much time with these people—more than with my friends.

PART-TIME CAREGIVER WANTED: WILL TRADE FOR ROOM

I had been advertising for two months. I really needed a second housemate for the evening shifts. My one housemate was pulling double duty and getting burned out by the routine. Unfortunately, the Thanksgiving and Christmas holidays were tough times to find someone in transition. Different friends helped out by volunteering nights and sleeping on the couch.

I knew that swimming somewhere in the pool of newspaper applicants were capable people who were dedicated to service, cheerful, and intelligent conversationalists. Unfortunately it was one extreme or the other, as a long-time quadriplegic once told me. The average length of stay for housemate caregivers was six months, before their lives opened to something else. I came to see my house as a way station, a place of respite for people to catch their breath and get their feet on the ground.

YES, I CAN DO EVERYTHING

The newspaper advertisements would bring various strangers to sit in front of me for intuitive assessment. Was this the person who could be responsible and learn my evening care routine? Was this the person with whom I could casually converse about politics or movies while going about the set tasks? Was this the person who could get along with two other housemates, four nurse aides and twenty volunteers? Was this the person who could be trusted to do all the right things in case of a medical emergency? Could I decide all of this in a one-hour meeting? Maybe there was an alien inside me, keeping me sane.

I had many delightful, competent people answer newspaper ads for work. But I've got to admit to the flipside and give brief descriptions of some of my other live-in caregivers. Let's see… there was the arsonist, a closet alcoholic who lived on Tic Tacs, the primadonna who couldn't boil an egg, the blackmailer, the thief, and a woman who kept bringing home men that were sleeping on the beach, proclaiming them her new best friends (three weeks after one such "friend" appeared, my television disappeared). Another sang songs to keep the voices out of her head and there was a passive aggressive fellow who gave much more than was asked of him, as long as he could lose it every four months and rage around the house late at night like an out of control alcoholic.

But the worst-case caregiver was the "perfect person." They would interview presenting tremendous credentials and experience. They were usually friendly, outgoing and assertive about their aim of helping people. They would make tremendous improvements by cleaning and fixing up the house.

Then they wanted more of my time. The "perfect person" would go "above and beyond the call" to do things for me and if I wasn't effusive with gratitude, they got sullen. These people had an intense craving for appreciation and validation, probably since childhood, and took service jobs as a means to that end. The situation usually turned out to be disagreeable and they had to leave. It was unfortunate when someone who I thought could be a reliable caregiver turned out to be a person who needed more of my care and attention than the situation required. I couldn't parent them; I had to be able to rely on their professionalism.

Other quadriplegics on Maui had similar "war" stories. Since this is an island of transient people, potential caregivers usually came from a pool of people who were financially desperate, emotionally wounded, or illegal aliens who couldn't officially work. (Oooh. There's that alien thing again.) As a sad comment on our times, a local social service agency would even pay to have a police report run on any prospective live-in caregiver.

WE HAVE SEEN THE ENEMY, AND THEY ARE US

Many of my experiences with housemates seemed surreal to me. I wasn't used to living with people who didn't tell the truth, or more accurately, didn't know the truth of what drove them. Many great thinkers have called this eclipse of truth the "shadow" side of life.

These people weren't evil; they came from all walks of life and were scared, abused or wounded souls. Any malevolence from them had at its source emotional pain and a fear of survival. I felt compassion for them, because they were really more disabled than I.

WHO GOES FIRST?

The more time I spent with these challenging people, the more I could see the reasons for their pain. A couple of times housemates opened up and told me of their horrific childhood experiences. Knowing their history drained out of me any initial, irrational fear.

I suddenly had room to see the spark of life they'd been protecting from years of trauma, that spark of God within the thickened shadows of their persona. Had I not been forced by paralysis to start a communal house, I never would've seen through my own fear of "those" people.

Honestly talking with someone can help break the vicious cycle of fear that keeps us all segregated in our protective castles. Somehow, by just spending enough sincere time with people who make you uncomfortable in some large or small way, you can't help but be inspired and have your life changed.

Two hours' volunteering at an AIDS clinic will get one closer to God than praying all day in church. Princess Diana would sneak her two sons out at night to spend time with homeless people sleeping under bridges. That woman changed Britain forever.

By practicing acceptance of people unlike myself, I was humbled to see how deep and pervasive original prejudices were in my life. Like a microcosm of society, I found myself in a small, ever changing household unit, practicing trust and normalcy. I still tied up my camel, though.

If a caregiver turned sour and we'd gone as far as we could, then that person had to leave. I needed the professional support of caregivers, not people I had to emotionally maintain. So we would part company, but usually changed for the better.

POSSESSION OBSESSION

There was a time in my life that if anything seemed practical, I rationalized its purchase. There was always something else to buy for my photographic business. I thought nothing of buying a new computer every year. Television commercials had me convinced that I just couldn't live without owning a ____. I even bought a Veg-O-Matic.

Sometimes we don't own things; things own us. Consumers can so easily be consumed, because possessions demand care and attention. I never realized how much time and energy I spent maintaining my "stuff." My car demanded that I change its oil. The carpet insisted that it be vacuumed. The fish needed to be fed, the garden watered. The piano would play if it wasn't tuned, but it would torture you. Quietly, slowly, seductively, I lost much of my free time to taking care of my things.

After my injury, most of my possessions seemed silly, and I awoke from their hypnotic control. With quadriplegia, you have to plan and direct people to do things for you. For the first time in my life, I couldn't handle or maintain most of my things. I had to ask others to maintain the bulk of my possessions, which grew very tiresome. If there was a little project, like hanging a picture on the wall or painting a chair, I had to wait until the next volunteer came to the house. Not only could I not mop up a glass of spilled milk, I had to roll in it until someone came by. Even directing the dusting of the trophies on the mantle got to be too tedious. The easiest and least expensive thing to do was to adopt a Zen lifestyle.

I had two huge garage sales and said goodbye to 90 percent of my worldly goods—NordicTrac, mountain bike, car, garden tools, etc., etc., etc. All the mementos went into storage boxes and I went into withdrawal. Who was I? Saying goodbye to all those possessions left me feeling naked. Saying goodbye to a lot of my camera equipment, dear old friends indeed, had me shaking. It was just like withdrawing from a powerful, all consuming drug (good riddance, though, to the Veg-O-Matic).

At first I went through moments of mourning, but then looked up to see a world with a gentler, richer gait. With more time and attention, I could sense things I never had before. I could hear the sounds of the neighborhood and pick up its subtle patterns. My neighbor's car accelerated, saying he was late for work. The neighborhood cat was on schedule, making its rounds and delicately crunching the dried leaves under my window. Sounds had a greater spectrum of richness. The colors were richer in trees. Being able to let go of possessions was truly a tremendous gift of time and energy, *because I wasn't spending hours shopping or earning money to spend*!

URGE TO MERGE

No matter what our philosophical backgrounds, we can all agree that bodies are meant to interact with the physical world. To twist, lift, throw, stack, dust, repair, caress, sweat, and build a pyramid or two is what our gene pool is all about. Let's put order in the universe!

One of my favorite kid memories was being awake after midnight one sweltering, humid evening in July. Half naked, fresh from a hot bed that wouldn't let me sleep, my feet wallowed in the cool, damp grass of the backyard. Thick schools of warm, yellow fireflies danced in choreography around me, accompanied by the cricket chorus. I pressed my bare chest and open arms into the boughs of a peach tree dripping with ripe fruit and inhaled deeply. Overwhelmed, my senses sent me swooning.

It has been said that angels, for all their glory, are envious of humans because we're born to this tactile, sensation-rich, physical world. Being in a wheelchair gave me a fresh, child-like enthusiasm for "manipulating matter." I appreciated the wisdom of learning new ways to interact with the physical world around me. With that came a renewed enjoyment of this glorious Eden all around us. Now I understand why I was always craving apples. It's a good thing Hawaii doesn't have any snakes.

12

HOMELAND SECURITY

My new house not only had a roll-in shower, but a deck with a view! At long last, I had a permanent home that fit all my needs. It only took eight years!

A fter a quick hello the realtor said, "We have got to do this today! There's been a lot of interest and it won't last long." My excitement was sobered as I rolled into a garage piled high with boxes, chairs, and a printing press. I had a deep knowing, which became an ache of understanding, that the next six months of my life would be frenzied and turned completely upside down—all for a good purpose, but still, it would be challenging.

I was in the throes of searching for a house in the cooler, dryer area of Maui. I had to move out of my small, cramped house in the moldy, rainforest section of this 30-mile-long island. The house was bad for my health (like having to shower outside), and not a lure for quality housemate caregivers, with its tiny bedrooms and limited privacy.

The ideal environment was 10 miles away, in the higher-altitude region of Maui's Haleakala volcano. There weren't many houses in that area, and finding an affordable one in the paper was impossible, because the good ones never even made it to the "Classifieds." I asked all the realtors to give me the first crack. After six months they all forgot—except for one.

"We have to get an offer in today," she said, stating the obvious. The house was fresh on the market and priced to sell. House buyers were crawling all over it like 6 a.m. shoppers at a flea market. It was a great house, with almost every aspect lovingly refurbished by the church group that owned it.

Placed at the exact center of a 2-mile radius that I thought was perfect for weather, drive time, modern telephone exchange and most of all, a terrific, 20-mile view across a valley to Maui's other volcano (don't worry, they're long dormant), the house was definitely worth going after.

With enough bedrooms for housemate caregivers, open architecture for easy wheelchair maneuvering and a fully accessible bathroom with a roll-in shower, I said, "Yes! Let's go for it!" It didn't matter that I was originally just looking for a rental and didn't have the money to purchase a home. All I had to do was step onto the roller coaster, fasten my seat belt and hang on.

Financing was the challenge. Only days were left in my escrow hold on the new house. I was fiercely committed to moving out of my tiny old place. In fact, I'd already given notice. I even had temporary access ramps built at the new home before knowing if the deal would close. My actions sound foolish, but they had their foundation in my reasoned, do or die determination. Finally, the banks agreed.

My brothers and sisters in the Midwest had squeezed together the down payment. One sister and her husband even mortgaged their retirement income properties, which meant I finally had to forgive her for telling Dad I was brewing wine out in the well house when I was fourteen.

I couldn't believe the house was really mine. At first I felt like the barking dog that finally catches the car it's been chasing for so long. Holding the bumper in my mouth I drooled, "Now what do I do?"

My regular lifestyle left me with only four hours of unscheduled, free time a day. In four days I had to move completely out of one house and into another. The thing I could do was to lift a telephone. I called in every favor and taxed every friendship to empty and clean the old house and fill up the new. Then two months of organizing, painting, construction, setting up garden irrigation, changing phone numbers, activating utilities and meeting the neighbors all left me rather fried.

I found myself on Thanksgiving Day writing from that same garage, newly painted. The previous owner's clutter had been replaced with my own, along with my office desk, computer, and exercise equipment.

PERSPECTIVE
The ability to perceive things in their actual comparative importance

With my family as landlords, I was able to freely remodel the house for accessibility, which is a lot of work on an average American home. While in the thick of remodeling, it seemed like every waking moment I was putting out fires. In the midst of the frenzy, I fell into a crack and out of time.

"You go ahead, I'll wait here," I said to my friend in the parking lot of Eagle Hardware. I was on yet another errand to get remodeling supplies. The list of items was short and I didn't want to take the time to unstrap and lower myself from the van, just to do it in reverse in a few minutes' time. So I waited in the van.

Strapped down firmly onto the center of the floor, reclining in my chair as though in a La-Z-Boy, I stared at the ceiling with nothing to do. Couldn't reach the radio or see outside. Outdoor sounds were muffled because the windows were closed. The van was like an isolation tank without water.

An internal list of agendas connected with the house scrolled past my closed eyes. These "have to dos" and "you'd better not forgets" had been consuming every waking moment, and I was deeply tired of their company. I came up with a novel idea—just tell them to go away!

"Come back when I'm at the computer and can write you down," I silently yelled to them. They didn't listen. They kept circling my sphere of attention with their demands, until a scream exploded out of me in frustration. I probably sounded like a car alarm in that parking lot.

Quiet followed. Without those two clamoring for my attention, the "worries" then surfaced. They too were summarily marched onto the back burner, along with the lists craving to be check marked. I sensed my quiet serenity again, the old friend that I'd come to know from deep meditation. Then the real seduction came next.

I was flooded with inspiring ideas, answers to questions, and better ways to do things. Within a minute I realized that these good things were equally distracting! The epiphanies and insights were hard to set aside.

The warmth in the van then took my attention. My body was tired and then... I was asleep. A nearby car honked, waking me from my catnap. Feeling refreshed I opened my eyes, not to see the ceiling of the van, but a scrolling list of things to do and remember, with attendant worries and inspirations. They were like children jumping the gun on a promised treat.

"Not now, we had an agreement," I protested. They slowly faded away and again, the warmth of the van prevailed. "I should have asked her to open the windows," I thought.

Then my body jumped up and took center stage. I became aware of the pain in my leg, the sounds of the parking lot, and the growl in my stomach. A cascade of other physical sensations made me vividly conscious of an incredibly rich moment.

In that sliver of time, seconds really, I realized the pain in my leg was just a small part of the cacophony of sensations happening every moment. If I focused on the pain, it would become my whole world—a painful world. If I focused on the never ending list of "to dos," I'd never get off the squeaking wheel in the cage. If my worries took center stage, I'd crave only safe routines. But if I could practice experiencing what was happening right then in the moment, without prejudice, I wouldn't feel disabled or deprived.

I was a part of the rich tapestry of life. Everything in sight and memory had richer colors. No part of the webwork was more or less important than another. My injury made complete sense. With this revelation came a deep contentment and renewed excitement about living this challenging lifestyle of mine.

This is an old story. Saints and sages have forever been telling us to slow down enough to stop the inner dialog that's yapping away like a nervous tour guide. This inner mind talk was a subtle director in my life, demanding obedience; and I usually didn't notice it was there. Often it would take a series of synchronous events to send me to a moment out of time and away from the chatter, which refreshed my spirits and reset my life's compass.

In March of 1969, a friend of mine was taking a walk—not around the block, but the planet—a space walk. Astronaut Rusty Schweikhart was inspecting the outside of the lunar module during NASA's *Apollo 9* mission. While flying weightless in a bulky space suit, traveling hand over hand on the outside of the ship, he was asked by Mission Control to stop moving. A fellow astronaut was filming Rusty from an open hatch, and the camera had jammed. Every minute of every space flight is dedicated to some activity, but while the camera was being repaired, Rusty had nothing to do but weightlessly wait. For the first time in the mission, he stopped. The ceiling of his van was the beautifully colored sphere of Earth. Within those few timeless moments, he had a life changing experience that would later direct him into the ecology and citizen diplomacy movements.

As Rusty so aptly summated, "When you go around the Earth in an hour and a half, you begin to recognize that your identity is with the whole thing. And that makes a change. From where you see it, the thing is a whole, the earth is a whole, and it's so beautiful. You wish you could take a person in each hand, one from each side of the various conflicts and say, 'Look. Look at it from this perspective. Look at that. What's really important?'"

THE MILLENNIUM

The last two months of every year are always incredibly active for everyone, except for the middle of the week between Christmas and New Year's Day. In this time between the "doings" of Christmas and New Year, I always hope that at the stroke of midnight on December 31, everyone celebrates being in the same "moment."

At the turning of the millennium there may have been blowing of horns or kissing, but essentially, millions of us joined in celebration of a once-in-a-lifetime moment. This special sliver of time, filled with the totality of Life, could also be considered an average moment. Then the next morning, there would be another "average moment," sweet and full of everything we need. If we continued adding them together like a string of pearls, they would give lie to the voices of fear and lack. This momentous beauty could be the daily momentum for the rest of our lives.

On millennium New Year's Day, I practiced the fine art of doing nothing with my full attention. Nothing happened but Life itself.

13

VANTASTIC

*After the electronic doors flew open, I unloaded myself from the van of my dreams.
Countless hours of effort and many fundraisers went into manifesting
this marvelous machine.*

CAR-MA

I felt like a broken record. Ever since my injury, I'd been talking about getting a van that I could drive, and had many fundraising benefits in this quest. This is the story of how I got control of the other physical vehicle in my life.

Some people call their physical body their vehicle. I guess that's so. It gets up and goes about the planet protecting that invaluable spark of life inside. Yet there's another vehicle of life, on which we often agree a *Blue Book* value—our cars.

These vehicles are a major part of our lives from the time of our first ride home from the hospital. Our teenage cravings for a certain make and model deeply embed these vehicles into our lives. We nurture our cars like children and shed a tear when they depart. They give action to our impulses and expand our worlds beyond the horizon.

Growing up outside of Omaha, I was able to legally drive at the age of thirteen (long story). I learned how to drive in an incredibly huge Plymouth; it floated on soft springs and drove like a boat. At fifteen, with my friends hiding in the back seat, I would sneak the car out of the driveway late at night and fly down the new interstate system. These were the only times I ever saw a car break 100 miles per hour.

The first car I owned was a Ford Mustang, my second a Rambler. Then I went on to a Volkswagen, switched to a new Chevy station wagon, and then moved on to an old Toyota station wagon, with a high ceiling that fit my tall, lanky frame. I also had two motorcycles in my vehicle lineage, but never in a million years did I imagine I would crave a big, fat, full-sized van.

After my injury, the first six months of my new life saw me in the passenger position of my Toyota station wagon. I was poured into my seat by three people and tended to fall over whenever we turned right. My manual wheelchair lay on its side in the back.

Since I only had the strength of half my arm muscles, I felt handicapped in my manual chair. When I graduated to an incredibly huge power chair, I never left the house because I didn't want to sacrifice the speed, agility, and security of my wonderful new electric wheelchair. So one year after my injury, I decided it was time to buy a van with a lift. Without resources, I got resourceful.

A Rusted Servant

The short life of my first van was described in an earlier chapter. It burned up on its maiden voyage, although the chairlift and raised roof were salvaged. The insurance settlement wasn't enough to cover a full replacement. While I tried to figure out what to do, I was given my second van—an old, liquid propane breathing, seating for a dozen, people moving transporter, similar to one you would take from the airport, but this one was from the era of prop airplanes. Poor suspension caused it to waddle down the road. It did have a chairlift, though, for which I was grateful. I was also proud of my friends, who without complaint jumped into the cockpit to steer this old whale of a van.

One year later I had an offer from the local community college auto shop instructors. They would transfer my adaptive equipment to a replacement van for free, if I could find one by the beginning of summer vacation, which was two weeks away. So I took the money I had and bought my third van, an '83 Ford Econoline. The "Boys Of Summer" donating their time made this conversion affordable. I gave the old whale to a quadriplegic mother of three. At last, her whole family could travel and picnic together. Eventually that whale would come ashore to die, and my third van would constantly try to follow it to the beach.

This old van, it drives slow,
yet I love it even so,
with a tick tick tock,
rocker engine gonna blow,
this old van has gotta go.

Van number three had over 200,000 miles on her, a second engine and a lot of rust. I gave up repairing the air conditioner and she never did have a heater. A phantom in the charging system kept me from going out at night for a year. Around thirty people courageously drove her as volunteers. They all got merit badges, although one of them tried to enter a parking garage built for economy cars. The bubble top roof leaked profusely following that collision, but still the ol' van ran.

Much of Maui was off limits to me because I didn't have confidence in the van's old engine. It was too tired to climb Haleakala, our ten thousand feet high neighborhood volcano. The far side of the island had too many narrow, curvy roads for my comfort, in case of a breakdown. So for five years I limited myself to the flatter, safer, central part of the island. I had a three-hour window in the afternoons when visiting friends would take me to doctors' appointments, shopping, or the movies. I would then scurry home and turn into a pumpkin at 6 p.m. Even so, a better van was at the bottom of my list of priorities. First came fundraising events for medical treatment and exercise equipment. Then, a better house to live in was essential. So I got used to the limited range of good ol' van number three.

TRAVELING BLOOPERS

Once, outside of a movie theater, I was trapped inside the van because the lift wouldn't lower to the ground. It was a Sunday and there was no one to call for repair, so my volunteer drove me back home. Once we got there, my driver ran over to the boys at the local fire station, two blocks from my house, and asked if they would pop over and help lift me to the ground in my power chair. Eight of them piled into their largest fire truck and squeezed into my tiny driveway. "Can't be away from our truck you know," said the captain as he coordinated my rescue from the van. I rolled off the partially deployed lift like I was walking a gangplank, trusting that I would roll off the edge into their hands and slowly sink to the ground. Well I did, and was greatly relieved, throwing thanks all around. Under the flashing red lights the captain said, "No problem. We do it for cats all the time."

Another occasion—it was dusk as a friend and I left the movies. A thirty-minute drive became an epic adventure when the alternator quit charging the battery. We only had the power already stored in the battery to get home. The engine would slowly eat this power. No problem, except that soon we would have to turn on the headlights.

We raced the cool, gray shadows that flowed down our volcano, Haleakala. Halfway home, in the small sugarcane town of Paia, oncoming traffic started flashing their lights—only three more miles to go. We turned on the parking lights, dimmed the dashboard, and killed the radio. The moon was out, so we could just see the road. We were on a curving rural road without streetlamps, so whenever we saw the headlights of an approaching car, we too would flip ours on until they'd passed, and then quickly switch them off again. Suddenly, the engine began to falter. Revving up the RPMs helped get us around the final curve and we coasted into the driveway at last. The engine immediately died.

I always tried to make it home in my own van, even under duress, because in the power wheelchair there was no other way to get home. No buses, no taxis and no sidewalks (my chair could roll six miles on a full charge). One time however, I had no choice.

Coming home from a movie again (hmmmm), my volunteer driver and I lost all power and coasted to the side of the road. Passing friends recognized the van and knew something was wrong. Five different groups of people attempted a rescue and failed, but at least we had a little roadside party while waiting for AAA. My wheelchair would have to be towed with the van, and I would have to get by with my back-up manual chair until the van was repaired. Night was falling, and I was stuck with being poured into a little car. Thankfully, a friend's van appeared and everybody lifted my vacated power chair through its sliding door. I was so relieved that my chair could follow me home. My van went into a dark parking lot overnight and was fixed the next day.

Old van number three was dying. It was time to buy a new one that would last the rest of my rolling life. It was also time to own a vehicle I could drive myself. With the help of friends and family, it was possible. But first we had to have some fun.

FUND RAISING

The knot in my stomach was the size of a grapefruit. Would everything be done on time? The caterer, volunteers, a dance band and three hundred other people would be converging on the country club ballroom in a couple of hours, and I wasn't ready. I was on the phone putting out tactical fires while a graphic artist friend was on my computer finishing up the benefit program. He still had several pages to go, and then we needed to make two hundred photocopies at Kinko's. Time was ticking...

We were setting up a "Sadie Hawkins" dance with food, a band, and "dates" for auction. Lil' Abner's Dogpatch was the theme, with a Daisy May look-alike contest. I was the co-host and nervous as a cat. Another friend was trimming my hair and comforted me with the reminder, "Don't worry Michael, things always work out."

Four hours later...

"Attention! Attention! May I please have your attention?" The crowd was noisily chattering with energy after the music had faded from the last dance. "I am handicapped!" I yelled into the microphone. "I am handicapped! And you can cure me." The room quieted down with curiosity. "I am transportationally disabled. Without public transportation on the island, I get out into the world on my own all too rarely. Your support at this benefit is raising funds for the purchase of a van—a van that I can drive myself!"

That's a scary thought: a quadriplegic driving a van! Buying a van with a chairlift, automatic doors, hand controls and a lowered floor would open a new life for me. It was time to become a teenager again and sweat buckets the morning of my first driver's exam.

I invited the sweaty dancers into the next room to place bids on the one hundred and fifty dates that had been donated for auction. These people had kindly and graciously offered themselves to be sold to the highest bidder. They packaged themselves with donated boat trips, picnics, helicopter rides, and candle-lit gourmet dinners on the beach, complete with the sound of violins weaving into and out of the lapping waves.

This took courage.

"What if no one bids on me or I'm bought by someone I'd normally never want to spend time with?" questioned some of my friends who'd agreed to be up on stage for the live auction bidding.

I gave them their answer as I spoke to the audience before the auction began. "We are here tonight with the innocence of times past. This is an opportunity for some of you to spend a few hours of quality time with a stranger or a casual friend. You may be surprised at your similarities. We all have beating hearts and a story to tell."

When the handsome doctor took the stage and offered an aerial tour of Maui in his private plane—to fly the highest bidder to a remote airport for a picnic lunch on cliffs overlooking the ocean—the bidding exploded.

More than four hundred people put some sort of time, energy or money toward this benefit, and yet no one was overburdened. In fact, it was just the opposite. Many volunteers commented on how much they'd received because of their participation.

The bottom line is that when we give to each other we bring more compassion into the world. Caring for people is one of the glues that hold society together; another is genuinely listening to each other. These simple actions hold great value for both individuals and society.

WILL YOU BE MY VALENTINE?

The next benefit had a different theme—Valentine's Day. In addition to a hot dance band and a food table loaded with exotic desserts, we had another "date auction." Some of the dates were as simple as a lunch affair, others as elaborate as a pack-mule excursion down the slopes of Haleakala volcano. How much would you have paid for a sunset ocean swim followed by a romantic, sit-down dinner for two on a moonlit, white sand beach?

Maui is a small island inhabited by very busy people. My benefit dances brought out the cream of her society, great people with big hearts. They routinely attended my galas and many said it was the best party of the year, probably because it was the only time they got to see so many old friends in one place.

All together, we raised $14,000 that evening for a drivable van worth $43,000. I loved the whole idea of people having fun while raising money for a good cause. I had a good cause—a van that I could drive. It was going to be expensive and I still needed a lot more money. So, the next year I began a new series of gala events. It's important to enjoy the journey, isn't it?

THE BLACK & WHITE BALLS

Out in the middle of the Pacific, we all got dressed up in our best black and white clothes and had a ball—The Black & White Ball. I produced five of these community events, which were dedicated to raise the rest of the money for a van that I could drive. People who hadn't surfaced for years came out of the woodwork for these events. Mix in a great dance band, good food, a silent auction, and terrific people, and fun just flowed all over the place.

This was one of my favorite postcards, sent out to promote the ball. Photographs from earlier events made up the collage.

The benefit balls were always successful, although they never seemed to get any easier to produce. I wasn't used to being the center of attention, and it was hard for me to ask others for help. Each year, dark, deep-rooted fears about not being good enough wriggled to the surface (where did those thoughts come from?). These slimy worms had to be scraped off my lens of perception daily and thrown into the compost heap. Every day I forced myself to keep working on the benefit. I usually teamed up with a fearless friend who kept me moving by example. Together we would ask for donations of food and items to auction at the event.

The benefit balls were my annual fifteen minutes of fame. I always choked back emotions when I saw the outpouring of generosity and appreciation for me. Yet at the same time people were saying "Thank you for the opportunity to give." In the beginning I thought they were joking. But in the end, I discovered a layer of our society that knew the rewards of giving to people, either materially or in service. They'd found the secret source of a meaningful life—helping others.

FOUR!

In the Midwest, the people in my hometown of Omaha have fundraising events with golf. I have no idea how it works—something about herding people around the course with a shotgun, forcing them to eat Mulligan stew at the end of each hole. Everyone convenes afterwards to sacrifice chickens and give doors as prizes to those who ate the most Mulligans.

My sisters rallied our family to put on another golf tournament for my benefit. A shotgun started everyone at the same time. Golfers could buy a Mulligan to reduce their score. Door prizes were given later at the chicken dinner. Everyone had fun except the chickens, and my van fund swelled.

There was a second side to this fundraising. A Maui foundation matched the funds raised in Omaha with an equal donation. I liked that two communities came together to help me drive again. This support was giving me a new life. In a way unique to wheelers, driving was the closest thing to walking. It was like being sixteen years old again, with a learning permit sticking out of my wallet. As I had with my father thirty years before, I would head for the deserted parking lots to relearn how to drive.

THE BIG AND TALL STORE

There are two things I'd like people to know about me. I'm incredibly good looking, and two meters high, or six feet, six inches tall. I love being tall. I could paint the ceiling, replace a light bulb and see dust on top of the refrigerator all without a ladder. Being a good guy I never sat directly in front of someone at the movies or picked a fight in school. I slept diagonally on king-sized beds and automatically ducked my head going through any doorway. When I was being carried across the sand to the ambulance after my injury, a volunteer surfer had to bring up the rear to support my dangling feet.

I always knew that I was a rare fellow who stood out above the crowd, my physical size being the most obvious sign. I once heard that any man over 6'3" comprises only one percent of the world's population. "One Size Fits All" never fit me.

I appreciated the irony of being a wheelchair sized 5'1" and still having to shop in the "Big and Tall Man" catalogs. My body frame remained intact and it showed by the size of my electric wheelchair. It was a monster. I'd even conceived how to use its black steel frame to attack the neighborhood pit bull if he ever got out of his yard and surprised me in mine.

I had a big chair. It would race effortlessly up my steep driveway with its 24-volt batteries, but once at the top it would stop in its tracks—The Road. The Road outside kept me under house arrest. My chair could be crushed out there by those huge, metal battlewagons, the SUVs! The only way out of my cul-de-sac was to ride high and with confidence in my own van.

THE BIG MAN DROP

"Next year," I always promised myself. "Next year I'll get a van that I can drive." I was sure the end of 2000 would be the purchase time because of heavy fundraising activity. The Omaha fundraiser had gotten me close enough to begin the ordering procedure. That was when I learned about the Big Man Drop.

With the new van, I didn't need to raise the roof as much as lower the floor. In order to see out of the windows, most wheelers needed to lower the floor six inches. Because of my great stature in life, I needed to lower the floor ten inches! This was rarely done and no one wanted to do the conversion. "It's too complicated and so few people want it," said the salesman on the phone while I wildly waved my arm.

After extensive searching, I found one company in Chico, California that would drop the floor of a full-sized Ford Econoline van the ten inches required to fit my frame. "But it would cost a lot more to reroute all the guts underneath," said the salesman.

This was called the Big Man Drop, a term which could also be used to describe my jaw as it fell open when I heard the cost. My $43,000 budget had just hit and run past the $50,000 mark. I was stunned and stammered to the salesman, "Are there any used vans with a Big Man Drop?"

"Haven't seen one in years," he said. "They are just so rare."

All I wanted was to have a semblance of a normal life, and I was still struggling for a basic goal that kept falling back as I was reaching forward.

My third van had been letting me know her time was about up. She couldn't wait until my next benefit to bring in the missing funds. She wanted to go to sleep.

THE NEW VAN

I couldn't wait any longer, so I bought a van from California, through the Internet, sight unseen, sans the extra equipment needed for me to drive. I saved $10,000 by buying a two-year old van to convert. It still had fifteen years of life in it. Funny thing; I knew I wouldn't replace it. This would be my final handicapped vehicle. The cure was coming down the highway way of life way before this van wore out. Until then, I had to sponsor one more benefit dance to raise the funds for the missing hand controls. In the meantime, I could at least be chauffeured in comfort and be able to see out of the windows again.

But the time was coming when I would once again be that sixteen year old with a learner's permit crumpled in his hand, being driven to a deserted parking lot. The driver's seat would unlock and relock into the empty passenger position. I would roll into the driver's position where a mechanical grip would grab the underside of my wheelchair and lock it into place. A special grip would hold my right hand to the steering wheel. My left arm would rest in a movable cradle—push forward to accelerate and pull back to brake. Both braking and accelerating would be superpowered and require minimal effort to move. I'd be styling.

Owning a drivable vehicle, along with having a secure and accessible home and all the computer equipment needed for my writing and photography, brought me up to the level I could call normal. To go beyond normal, I needed a sweetheart.

14

"DANGER! DANGER, WILL ROBINSON!"

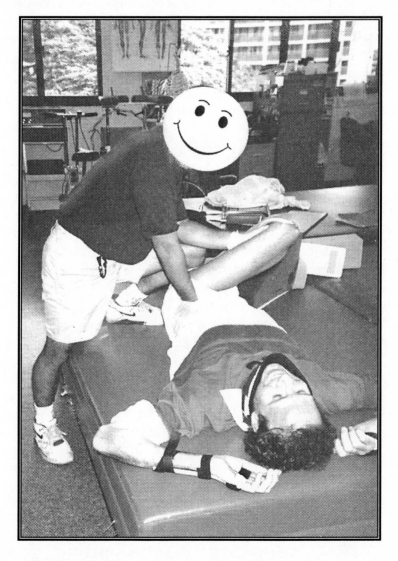

This is traditional physical therapy for people with paralysis and degenerative diseases, and those who've suffered a stroke. It was important, but I knew there had to be more.

One of my favorite shows as a kid was the camp TV science fiction epic *Lost in Space*. Every week the young Will Robinson set out with his trusty robot, who would warn him of impending danger. Boy and bot survived each week by avoiding dangerous situations because of this robot's exceptional radar.

When you're paralyzed, there are dozens of dangerous things that you might experience—skin breakdowns, bladder infections, torn rotator cuffs (we weren't made to walk with our arms), bouts of depression, psychotic caregivers, bone fractures, muscle contractions, crosswalk speeders, etc.—so you really develop a sixth sense of how to protect yourself.

We are all born to die. *But* in the meantime we get to live! To live a life completely overflowing with joy, absurdly rich in experience, and effervescent with love for ourselves and others is our birthright!

Sometimes we need a brush with death or intense pain to cause a wounding that will guide us to bloom into a full appreciation of life. Many fruiting seeds require a brutally cold winter to crack their protective hull. Other systems need fire to bring them into new life.

Young soldiers who go fearlessly into battle are usually no older than twenty. Their bravado is sobered after their first brush with death. For most of us, until we hit thirty we don't really believe anything bad could ever happen to us. But something about seeing that first wrinkle or having the realization that a body just cannot operate on four hours of sleep is a wake-up call that we're all born to die. With that rite of passage tucked under our belts, it becomes easier to rule out choices that can hurt us, like buying a dirt bike.

Wise parents inculcate their children early on with the understanding that life is precious and teach them not to squish ladybugs and fireflies or kill rabbits (although cockroaches and mosquitoes do need to die). Children with a healthy sense of their own mortality will make wiser decisions at every stage of their lives.

But sometimes you have to take a chance and risk harming your body for a greater good. You have to do something bold that might help you and trust that it won't be damaging. It helps during these times to have wise counsel looking over your shoulder. You might think I'm crazy, but this is what I had to do while living on The Edge...

WOULD YOU LIKE STARCH?

Many spinal cord injuries do not physically sever the tissue in the spine. All that has to be done is a wicked twist or an overstretching to traumatize the tissue into swelling. Have you ever twisted an ankle and been amazed at how swollen it could get? The spinal cord can also massively swell but is limited by its protective home, the bony spinal column. Unfortunately, swelling chokes off blood supply and the tissue dies. The first thing to go is the insulation around the nerves; everything short-circuits and communication is lost.

If nerve damage happens in a peripheral limb such as an arm, the nerves will slowly regenerate to full function. Tissue in the spinal cord doesn't want to do that. I guess the body hasn't evolved yet beyond thinking that if someone has a spinal injury, that's it; the individual is toast. Better they die quickly, because there wouldn't be enough time to heal or escape before a wild animal came along to eat the sitting duck.

The only FDA approved therapy for acute spinal injury is carried in all ambulances. As soon after injury as possible, anti-inflammatory drugs are given in order to reduce the spinal cord's suicidal tendency to swell. I'm sure for some people they save the day. I got paralyzed.

When I got home from the rehab hospital three months later, I could barely control my arms. My hands flopped about and I used braces to keep them up. I was told by the powers that be that I would get more functional return as my spinal cord shrank to its original size, but it could take over two years for that to happen. I wondered if I could speed that up.

An alternative health doctor told me about a process that could dramatically reduce the swelling in my spinal column. It was not an FDA approved regimen, however, so I would have to go underground. He could prescribe the drug for me, but I would have to find someone else to inject it. This was more than just a shot—it was an I.V. drip! A bag of saline solution would be infused with vitamins to buffer in the primary ingredient, DMSO—commonly known as dry cleaning fluid.

I would have to sit for the drip every day for a month. The only side effects, the doctor promised, would be intense body flushing and heat while on the drip, an obscene odor of garlic on my breath for the full month, and an arm full of holes.

The idea was to systemically flush my whole body with DMSO, which has an astringent effect on tissues, chemically squeezing from them any excess fluid. Any swelling in my spinal cavity would be reduced in this one-month period, rather than waiting a whole two and a half years.

I had to try it. Even though it was an underground procedure, if I could get more return functionality I would go for it; I had to. In the early days and months following my injury, I often felt I was living in a nightmare, desperately trying to wake up.

The pharmaceutical was very expensive, but many friends helped in the purchase. A private duty nurse would have charged $1,500 to do the entire procedure. As it so happened, one of my housemate caregivers was an out of work nurse, and he volunteered to poke my arm for free.

Before starting the regimen I cut back on one of my medications because I was afraid it would conflict with the new procedure. It was at that point that I learned my first big lesson about medication—never abruptly stop a drug your body is used to, i.e., addicted to. Withdrawals can be bizarre.

The night before the beginning of the Big Drip was the end of my fifth day without the drug Baclophen, a muscle relaxant. As I was talking to my out of work nurse caregiver that evening, I suddenly noticed the room pulling away from me. Was my hand moving the electric wheelchair backwards? Then it didn't matter. I didn't know where I was or who I was. What was I?

I could hear strange people talking outside the scope of my tunnel vision. I was transfixed on the stereo cabinet while trying to remember in the back of my mind what I was about to think. I knew it was important, and I was beginning to panic because I felt like my life depended on having a memory—any memory. Like a broken record, I was stuck with my present thought, stuck with my present thought, stuck with my present thought, stuck with my present thought, stuck with my present thought...

My breathing became labored. I had to get outside for fresh air. With my caregiver trailing behind, I frantically began searching each room for an exit. He was bound and determined to keep me away from the busy street outside, beyond the end of the driveway. He later told me that I was like a belligerent drunk, totally committed to getting outside, oblivious to anything outside of my narrow tunnel. He had even grabbed a wire cutter and followed me outside. "If you'd gotten too close to the street, I was going to cut the control wires on your power chair," he grinned.

In the cool of the night air, I remembered what I forgot to remember. I motioned my caregiver over and whispered "Rosebud," having just remembered the previous night's movie. I didn't know who or where I was, but at least I'd retained a sense of humor. Giggling to myself, I signaled him to come over again and whispered "Baclophen." Being a nurse he immediately understood why I'd gone out of my mind—Baclophen withdrawal. He gave me two and in thirty minutes I was back making bad jokes consciously.

I had no explicit medical knowledge that I needed Baclophen. It came from an intelligence deep inside me, a comforting presence that was always there during a crisis. I can't say for certain it was God. It seemed to be the essence of me, unfettered by worry or doubt or pain or fear. We first met in the ambulance departing the beach and heading into my new life, and it has shown up as a still, quiet voice easily heard during subsequent years. It isn't a demanding voice; I feel calm and succored when I listen to it. Did it take my old life falling away in order for my mind to be quiet enough to hear, or was it always available, just beyond the daily din of ordinary existence?

Unlike the little girl/voice in the movie *A Beautiful Mind*, my adviser seems to be aging and getting wiser with time. And yet it still thought squirting dry cleaning fluid in my veins was a good idea.

The next evening I began the I.V. drip. Thirty nights of poking, dripping, flushing, sweating, eating ice cream and radiating garlic passed—and the stuff really worked! I had a dramatic increase in muscle control. My left arm was transformed from a loose appendage to a viable, working arm. I could use it for hugging, and with the aid of my right arm, could use it to trap a cup of coffee in my hands and raise it to my mouth. I also regained articulation in my wrists and no longer needed braces to hold up my hands. I could wave hello, put on my reading glasses, or pick up a broad-handled spoon to feed myself.

The voice/intuition/feeling came up again in the following months when I read about an experimental therapy for paralysis using a European drug called Sygen.

THE SWISS DOCTOR

Medical explanation: at the site of neural injury, excessive quantities of excitatory amino acid neurotransmitters are released, which overstimulate associated amino acid receptors (i.e. receptor abuse) and neurons, leading to cell injury and death. Sygen prevents these toxic consequences without interfering with the normal physiologic functions of amino acid neurotransmitters on undamaged neural tissue.

Lay terms: toxins from damaged tissue eat up nerves, starting with their insulation. Sygen can prevent this from happening.

I had to have it. There was a controlled desperation to being brand new in the world of paralysis. I would try anything. Multiple fundraisers and donations underwrote two trips to the mainland for clinical therapy. It was all incredibly stressful and very expensive, but I had to do it; at least I had to know that I had tried. When I heard about Sygen, I knew I could figure out a way to get it. I had another purpose for my Black & White Ball fundraisers. Sygen was expensive.

My local doctor wrote a prescription for Sygen that went, along with requisite forms, to Switzerland, where it was manufactured. Since Sygen wasn't approved in this country, I needed a doctor in Switzerland to join my cause. I just happened to have one of those.

In the 80s I was hired by a small family from Switzerland to join them in their travels around the planet. They were looking for the best country to which to emigrate. At its head was a medical doctor. During two years of travel we became friends, and it was he who expedited the Sygen halfway around the world to me.

The Federal Express man helped me open the box. They were like liquid gold, all those bottles shimmering with promise. Break out the needles—we're drilling again.

Twice a day for a month we looked for fresh skin to poke on my shoulders and thighs. The thick, syrupy liquid would take its time oozing out of the thin needles. The large welts on my skin would go down in a couple of hours. I was very excited, and then...

Nothing happened. I didn't get any more improvements, but neither did I get any of the side effects, like premature balding. Oh, wait a minute... Two months after I began my personal trial of Sygen, I chalked it all up to experience and thanked the co-conspirators who had helped me. Subsequent clinical trials determined Sygen was best used within seventy-two hours after an injury.

I'm glad I tried it. I had then done all the heroic things I could think of doing. That made it easier to settle into "chopping wood and carrying water"—the day to day routines of paralysis. There was more than enough to keep me busy. Just maintaining my body was work enough. At that time, I had yet to get exercise equipment, a better van, a livable house, and a sweetheart. I was in excellent health, so I could settle in, pamper myself, and enjoy my friends and family.

15

THEY EVEN STOLE THE CAN OPENER!

Obstructions: I was absolutely positive, so sure I couldn't make it, that I didn't even want to try to get by this fireplug. At the urging of my beloved, I held my breath and squeezed by, with my outer wheels running along the edge of the curb.
This kind of obstruction in life is measurable. When it comes to people, you sometimes have to live with them to really know if they are friend or foe.

E veryone has to live somewhere, and most of us have to live with someone. If you're a quadriplegic, you probably have to live with someone to survive. If you're young, you live with your ily. If you're older, you may have a family of your own for support.

If you're single, you either live in a nursing home or have a larger home, with housemates as caregivers. Thanks to a HUD rental subsidy, I had a house with extra room for caregivers.

BOAT PEOPLE

She was fresh off the boat—literally. She and her boyfriend had been cruising the islands when he got a job offer on the mainland. They sold the boat and camped on a deserted beach for a few days. She read my "Help Wanted: Caregiver" classified and passed the interview. She was only twenty-two years old, but had a lot of experience as a caregiver. Usually I avoided hiring people fresh to the island, but I was getting desperate to fill a vacancy. No time to check references, so I went on intuition and gave her the job.

Two days before she was scheduled to come in, the new housemate telephoned to ask if her boyfriend could come as well. He'd been offered a better job on Maui and decided to stay. Time was running out, and I didn't have another replacement.

"OK, sure. I guess it will be all right," I said, crossing my fingers.

They moved in by emptying their van of all their worldly possessions and sleeping for the next two days. Then they started working around the house, and I thought all was well.

SOCIAL TRAINING WHEELS

It is a real art living with other people. I started by being part of a large Catholic family in the Midwest. I learned to eat very fast in order to get seconds. Hand-me-downs were the usual attire when we were small, and sharing a bedroom was the norm. This safe, nurturing environment infused me with the lifelong impression that people are good and loving.

I moved away for college into the attic space of a communal house near the Art Institute in Kansas City. Living in a garret was the thing to do for a starving artist. Seven people had to get along with each other and support the house. Every house member had one night each week to cook a meal for us all, a house chore, and an unspoken agreement to respect everyone else's personal space.

One of the house jobs, rotated every week, was going to the farmer's market on the weekend and buying everything in bulk for seven people—cheese, breads, milk, fresh vegetables, dry goods, fruits of the season, pure, fresh local juices, homemade yogurt, vitamins, and a huge spectrum of spices that were totally new to me. We all ate very simply and stayed very healthy.

One Saturday in spring we all jumped in the backyard and enthusiastically created a massive, communal vegetable garden. Working with the other household members to do this dirty job was fun because of our camaraderie and esprit de corps.

I was quite impressed by how inexpensive the cost of living could be when I invested my time in preparing food and buying in bulk—thus avoiding expensive processed foods. I learned to love the visceral satisfaction of beans and rice as my primary diet. No matter what happened with my career, I knew I could physically survive on a dollar's worth of beans and rice a day. I was also introduced to the joys of avocados, squash, sprouting seeds, soybean products and "hepin out" your neighbor, all in midtown Kansas City. I learned there how sweet a healthy extended family experience could be.

Shared living became a natural for me. I loved sharing expenses and buying food in bulk. It was empowering to know how happy and comfortable I could be living off of almost no money (artist's training). This was good training, because I eventually gravitated to living in upscale, high rent areas of the country, where I had to watch my pennies and share house and garden with other people.

The epitome of high cost of living is dear ol' Maui. I was sharing a mansion on the ocean with several friends and work colleagues when I injured my neck, further committing myself to living with housemates. At my level of quadriplegia, I needed a fair amount of help in a twenty-four-hour period.

I eventually settled in a four-bedroom, mountainside home on Maui's Haleakala volcano. Three of those bedrooms were traded out to people for their assistance. For fifteen hours of work per week, housemates got a bedroom, utilities, telephone, and cable. In exchange, they kept the house clean, did shopping, cooked meals, and helped me get to bed at night. It wasn't complicated work; in fact, it was rather easy. At the same time, it couldn't be considered a career, so I had a lot of turnover. Six months was a long time for someone to stay. One September, I reached the record shortest stay for a caregiver. Boat lady was in and out in seven days.

The first primary rule of the household was "don't steal food from each other." You could sample a bite for curiosity's sake, but not ever take something without asking. You could sneak a little milk for your coffee, but only once from each container. And when someone let you borrow food, you always had to replace what you took.

After the arrival of the boat people, I saw that someone had taken half my onion and placed the remainder in the hanging baskets bare naked, without even Saran Wrap. I groaned. That had never happened before, so it had to be boat lady or her boyfriend. They obviously didn't know the "food code." But forget food—that night they broke a universal rule of life called "no beating on your girlfriend." They had to go.

The next morning I called a quick house meeting to tell them that violence was completely unacceptable and they would have to leave the house by sundown. After a hasty acknowledgement, they spent the day sequestered in their bedroom, so the two other housemates got a chance to compare notes.

"From day one they were taking my food. I stopped bringing any home because I knew they would steal it. Eating out was getting expensive," said one.

"He was always abusive to her when you weren't looking, Michael. How do you think she got that bruise on her cheek?" filled in the other.

"We kept our distance when boat lady told us how much fun it was to shoplift," they continued.

Boy, was I out of the loop. My only insight was that I didn't trust boat man because he called me "Dude," "Chief," and "Bro." He seemed like a "talker" to me. We had rarely interacted that week.

THE OL' HEAVE HO

Going on 6 p.m. and still no movement from their room, so they were told they had two hours to vacate the house. Only then did the boat people start to pack—by stuffing the washing machine!

Just before the 8 p.m. deadline, I heard them packing up in the kitchen. I wondered if they were stealing food again, but it didn't matter; they were leaving! At 8:30 their van was backing up the driveway. They said they were going to camp out in a pasture to "find some mushrooms and have a good time." They could've stayed out there a week based on the amount of food they stole. Inspecting the kitchen after their departure, I saw that my fresh food had been decimated and my canned food reduced by half. I expected that, but I didn't expect them to steal my can opener!

Two days later, food stamps for them arrived in the mail. I was stunned. I'd never been exposed to people that lazy and self-centered. They had no excuse to be on public assistance. They both were young, healthy, childless, and turning down work! I'd overheard boat lady mention that her primary goal in life was to have babies, so she could do nothing but take care of them. Guess I dodged a bullet. She might have started to see me as one of those babies, figuratively. I'd been there before.

Some caregivers didn't have a sense of inner direction and purpose. They felt their lives only had meaning when they were playing the role of caregiver. I'd had caregivers like those and it soon felt icky. I would become their main focus, and if I didn't interact with them in the way they needed, their attitudes turned sour and mildly abusive. They would assume a passive aggressive nature and all of a sudden, I would be served burned toast! As with boat lady, I would tell them it was time to leave. As for more vulnerable folks, like the elderly infirm and children, minimum wage workers can smack them around when no one is looking (remember the baby cams?). These are extreme cases, but they happen too often by only occurring once.

CANARY IN THE COAL MINE

I felt like the canary in the coal mine, on the leading edge of a huge groundswell of baby boomers who would like to live at home in their elder years. My injury had given me a chance to experience being medically retired and living at home ahead of time. My housing arrangement gave me half the support I needed. The other half came from a state-subsidized nursing agency staffed with home health aides.

Anyone can become a home health aide with little to no training. Newspaper "Help Wanted" ads are asking for live-in caregivers, with "No Experience Needed." This is just the beginning. The baby boomers will be relying on home health assistance someday; their parents already are. The need will become so huge that desperate families will take anything they can get. I predict trouble ahead.

Our national healthcare system will need a dramatic overhaul. In its current state, only the wealthy can afford consistent, quality home health care. We have to make it an educational priority to train an army of home healthcare providers. Caregiving must become more than a minimum wage job with no benefits, no advancement, and no prestige. It should be elevated to the status of an esteemed, viable career choice.

On the whole, my experience with caregivers was good. Most of them were terrific people sincerely trying to make a difference in the world. But a few bad apples made me cautious—I lost my innocence. Rats. I became a better judge of character, though, a skill any of us would be wise to learn.

You don't have to reinvent the wheel of learning who would be a good caregiver for you or your loved ones. Others have gone before. One woman, June Price, has twenty years' experience in hiring caregivers, and has written a great book called *Avoiding Attendants from Hell*. I highly recommend it for its hard-earned wisdom. Below are a few points, stolen from the book jacket:
- Screening and interviewing techniques
- Training and hiring methods
- Avoiding pitfalls in working relationships
- Sample want ads, job applications, and live-in contracts.

By avoiding attendants from hell, what remains are the angels who are professional, ethical and kind. Our can openers will be safe.

MY SOAPBOX

I usually suspend judgment about folks because I know there are a lot of reasons why people do the things they do. But when their actions affect my life and I lose a can opener, then I have the right to speak out. So, here's a question: why don't public schools teach the basics—other than reading, writing, and arithmetic (and poorly at that)? How about ethics and morality? It wouldn't be that big of a deal to have one class each semester suggesting the framework for a constructive, happy life that respects all people and one's role in society. This isn't to be confused with teaching religion; it's just teaching our young how to interact with others in a way that builds a healthy society.

If parents aren't teaching these basic skills, then society must, for its own survival. We have to do more than let poorly made school videos teach conflict resolution or video games will come to life as tragically as at Columbine High School.

How are the fibers of our society strengthened by television's constant dramatization of people killing people? Children in America see twelve thousand simulated murders on television by the time they're fourteen years old. That number doesn't even include our old friend the video game. Violent video games enable violent options for the resolution of our children's problems. Got a problem with your teacher, parent, or a bully at school? Blast your way out! Violence in. Violence out.

We can't let our kids find self-esteem and life's meaning in drugs or expressing their sexuality. We can't continue the psychological wounding of our children, which leads to addiction. We can't afford to imprison multiple generations of crack addicts.

We are not elevating our children higher than our own generation! Elevation is the tradition of our species that got us to the moon and gave us the longest lifespan in the history of mankind. Sadly, we're standing on the shoulders of our children and grandchildren instead, crushing their spirits and their future for perverse motives—profit and indifference.

It's frustrating to watch the wasting of precious lives and social resources of a human lineage that first harnessed fire 800,000 years ago! Every one of our ancestors worked hard to survive and pass the torch of life on to another generation. Is the torch being dropped?

I hold out hope that unlike my boat lady housemate, the vast majority of our young women won't want to get pregnant just for kicks, and that if they do, they'll at least stay in school long enough to open opportunities other than those afforded to welfare mothers. And hopefully, the drug-selling young men in our society won't end up in jail with no opportunities except to be some big fella's girlfriend.

THE BIG KAHUNA SOAPBOX

My experience with the boat people validates my theory about the world's troubles. This really sounds presumptuous, but I've been thinking about it for twenty years now and am officially putting it down on paper. I'm not the first author, though, to write about a pandemic of self-destruction.

Dr. Wilhelm Reich wrote about a psychological concept he termed "The Murder of Christ Syndrome." He considered it to be an emotional plague systemic throughout the ages. Very simply put, some people get disconnected from the Source of Life, and go through a form of pathological withdrawal. They start hurting things, especially good people who shine so brightly it illuminates what's missing in their own lives.

Too many people in the world are disconnected from their Source. They have a spiritual hunger, a vacuum driving them to do rather dumb things out of an indiscriminate anger. We see their negative activities on the evening news every night. They're truly not relating to something life affirming. A suicide bomber is passionately connected to a movement, but it's definitely not a life affirming one. An Enron-style executive has a passion for his bottom line that is definitely not life affirming. There's a quote from Carlos Castaneda's book *The Power of Silence* that seems pertinent here. It says, "Having lost hope of ever returning to the Source of Everything, the average man seeks solace in his selfishness."

I have long noticed people who are in touch with this Source. They are happy, honest, loving people. They're excited about life and generously contribute to their communities. These folks are compassionate and strive to do good in the world. They come in all colors and religions, and have a single common denominator—they feel connected to something larger than themselves. These people of the Source (sorcerers) have an excitement for living life fully. Some call their Source God (by many names), and some call it being connected to their bliss (their life's calling). Others come to know their Source by having a beloved in their life (a soul mate).

They all are connected to something bigger than themselves, a Source of their being that feeds their soul. They overflow with love and cannot help but look around to see how they can be of service to humanity. These are the people who volunteer for good causes, engage consciously in their local church, or work passionately late into the night producing art that demands to come out. These are the people connected to their life affirming Source.

So... what disconnects people from the succor of their Source? Pain. Pure and simple, unresolved pain. Resolution and reconnecting to the Source gets trickier if the pain comes at the hands of another person—especially if you're a child.

Alcohol and the rest of the alphabet soup of addictive substances can dull the pain. The toughest thing in the whole wide world may be facing your fears, returning to the genesis of your disconnection, and going through the healing process.

In his book *The Power of Intention*, Dr. Wayne Dyer encourages the reader to face their fears by changing perspective and reconnecting to the Source. He writes, "Anything you experience as other than eternal is simply not life. It's an illusion created by your ego, which strives to maintain a separate address and identity from its infinite Source. This shift toward seeing yourself as an infinite spiritual being having a human experience, rather than the reverse—that is, a human being having an occasional spiritual experience, is loaded with fear for most people. I urge you to look at those fears and face them directly right now; the result will be a permanent connection to the abundance and receptivity of the universal Source."

In the previous section, the word "Source" was used many times. It's God, folks, and there have been thousands of different names throughout the ages to describe this universal, all pervasive force. Consider it an SUV—a Single Universal Value. If you're connected to the universal Source, is it as comfortable as sitting behind the wheel of a new SUV?

SINGULARLY UNCONSCIOUS VEHICLES

Everyone was getting them, even though they guzzled enough gas to keep us dependent on Middle Eastern oil supplies. I sure wished I could have an SUV! I wanted to pretend I had a deep and dire need to use my four-wheel-drive to save someone in a swamp or carry drinking water to front-line firefighters in the forest. What if it started to snow? I could go out and pull cars from the ditches. OK, stop Michael.

Fact is that most SUVs are used for the work commute, picking up the kids, and going to shopping malls—while inhaling gasoline. Unfortunately, the SUV mentality is killing our planet in all too many ways. The most popular vehicles in America, SUVs are notorious gas guzzlers. I'm embarrassed to say that my wheelchair van only gets fifteen miles per gallon, but I have a good excuse. It's the only way I can travel.

FUN FACTS TO KNOW AND TELL

A streamlined SUV is a luxury passenger shell on a high-powered truck frame. Since they're considered trucks, SUVs do *not* have to meet the fuel economy standard of passenger cars, and are lucky to get twelve miles to the gallon. SUVs also do not have to meet the safety standards of new passenger cars. People think they are safer in an SUV, but actually it's just the opposite.

The truck frame of an SUV is rigid. Hit a telephone pole and you better hope that the airbags work. A contemporary passenger car has a crumple zone that will absorb the force of impact before you even touch the airbag.

Unfortunately, the United States is not alone in shunning cars already in production that get sixty miles per gallon. Most middle-class

Chinese have or plan to have their own car, and they love SUVs! Problem is, they're not concerned about emission controls—yet. China has seven of the ten worst polluted cities in the world, and the winds blow eastward.

The West Coast is awash with carbon pollution from Chinese cars and coal-fueled power plants. If we burn more fossil fuels in our tanks, even more carbon goes up into the atmosphere. I won't bore you with details about global warming, but I will advise everyone not to buy beachfront property.

W.W.J.D.?

"What would Jesus drive?" is an evocative question put forth by the Reverend Jim Ball, director of the Evangelical Environmental Network. Some evangelical Christians have chosen to boycott SUVs because of the impact of their poor gas mileage on the environment. Ball urged consumers and automakers to start thinking of gas mileage as an ethical matter, duly noting that auto emissions are significant contributors to climate change (i.e. global warming).

"Somebody's got to represent the long-term future, and the long-term future doesn't get much market share. So we have to do it," stated John Briscoe, speaking for the National Council of the Churches of Christ.

These quotes are from an article by Katherine Ellison in the *Washington Post*. I'm always inspired to hear about small groups asking for change in vital areas. All too often, our environment has played the role of the innocent. And it's slowly being strangled. Three cheers for these and other groups that come forward to champion its survival—our survival. As the anthropologist Margaret Meade famously said, "Never doubt that a small group of thoughtful, committed people can change the world; indeed, it is the only thing that ever has!"

Individual commitments can have just as much impact. While driving around an area of Maui noted for its winding roads along cliff faces overlooking the ocean, a spectacular view commanded that my beloved and I pull off. There was just a little bulge on the narrow road for parking, so when a pickup truck also pulled over, we couldn't help but notice the driver's actions.

With a short broom and a scoop bucket, he went around collecting cigarette butts, beer cans, and other trash. He dumped the trash into a bulging, plastic garbage bag tied to the railing. Our open windows invited this gentle stranger to comment with a smile, "Ever since I started tying these garbage bags up, most trash doesn't get thrown off the edge of the cliff anymore."

That breathtaking view had no doubt pulled over many travelers, as it had us, and eventually, enough trash had collected on that spot for this man to take notice. He explained that years before, on his own, not as a county worker, he had adopted five curvy turnouts to protect and keep clean. Every day he made his rounds, every day he did more than he had to, every day he championed a beautiful view for unknown passersby to appreciate without the blight of garbage. This man was happy and connected to the Source of Life. He was changing the world all by himself.

So... what does all of this have to do with my being disabled? Well, since my injury, I've come to know some rather remarkable people. Some were wealthy, some poor, but all had a deep awareness of the human condition and acted on it. From volunteers who just appeared on my doorstep to Christopher Reeve and his wife Dana, who were on a mission to help change the world en masse, all could see that they could do something for someone other than themselves.

I have been picking on the SUV mentality as a case in point of one of the world's many disabling problems. We shouldn't gobble up the planet's resources and continue creating climate change just "because we can." Our grandchildren will call us the selfish generations (I apologize if I've gotten you angry). There are many, many, many more problems that subsequent generations are going to confront because of our choices. They will do it one person at a time, and it may take most of this century.

I wasn't a writer when I started the beginning of this book. My passion for writing has grown since my injury because of its impact on my gracious readership. Throughout the years, response letters and e-mails to my newsletter and web site have shown me that we're all going through similar emotional and physical challenges that bind us like a cocoon, yet promise a transformation. I can't raise millions for spinal cord research like the Reeves can, but I can do my part. If my writing can improve even one person's outlook on life, then I too am happy to be cleaning my section of the roadway of life.

16

I GOT THE ELECTRIC CHAIR

My new wheelchair could do marvelous things. In addition to lying out flat for a nap, I could raise my feet into the air to relieve pressure on my backside. I couldn't really read in this position, but I could see constellations in the ceiling tiles.
Other state-of-the-art machines could even climb stairs and raise the rider up to the eye level of walkers at a cocktail party. Some were four-wheel-drive, designed to travel on hiking trails. Would that make them SUV wheelchairs?

This chapter title sounds ominous enough, but really it describes an exciting moment in the life of someone paralyzed when their eyes widened and their hearts skipped a beat.

After I was first injured, I lay motionless for a month in the rehab hospital until finally being loaned a manual wheelchair. I got around by going in semicircles. My left arm was much weaker than my right arm. I would start out with the chair going straight and invariably curved to the left. After catching my breath, I would push with only my left arm to straighten the chair towards my destination. Blasting off again with both arms, I would go about five feet before curving to the left and hitting a wall. Then I pushed only the left-hand wheel to straighten out and begin again using both hands, trying to stay in the center of the hallway. This was a challenge at first, but I got used to it. Anything is better than lying in bed.

I spent the first six months back home rolling into walls and furniture until that spectacular day when they delivered my first electric wheelchair. I felt like a kid again, looking at my first bicycle under the warm glow of the Christmas tree. The power chair was all black, except for some chrome accenting and teal-colored plastic hubcaps. It cost as much as an average new car, but unfortunately didn't have that glorious, new car smell.

There was celebration at my house. A number of friends came over to watch me be transferred into the new electric wheelchair and take my first ride. The seat cushion was made of air bubbles, and the wheels were small and connected to powerful motors. Well, only the back wheels were motorized—the front wheels were like grocery cart casters that thankfully didn't wobble. Directly under the seat sat two very heavy, car-sized batteries that were permanently sealed to prevent acid from escaping if I ever tipped over. But there were "wheelie bars" on the frame to keep me from tipping over backwards. That chair had enough power to go up a very steep hill or pop up and over a curb.

I couldn't believe the manual when it boasted I could go over twenty miles on a single charge. If I were to have such an adventurous day, and drained the battery, there were levers in the back that could be pulled, disconnecting the motors. Then the chair could be pushed.

So, how does a quadriplegic control a 250-pound vehicle? At the end of my left armrest was the controlling joystick and other electronic switches. This joystick's ancestor ended up on the moon. Back in the 70s, the *Apollo* program's lunar rover had to be totally controlled with one hand. A dedicated team of NASA engineers designed the forerunner to the joystick on my electric wheelchair. (This was relayed to me by my friend Gerry Carr, an astronaut who was part of this team.)

Once the power to the electric motors was turned on, the joystick responded to my touch, and my spacecraft could reach the cruising speed of a fast jogger. I stayed away from the wheelchair's high-end speed; too scary. I was quite content to sit on what I felt was a king's throne and meander about the house, sidewalks, and stores. I did have to stay away from the sand of Maui's many beautiful beaches. I would instantly get stuck. One beach park does loan out a waterproof wheelchair with Michelin Man foam tires that goes from the parking lot to the ocean.

For the first time since my injury, my whole body moved when my brain asked. By using just my shoulder muscles and half my arm muscles, I was able to move the joystick with incredible dexterity.

My heroes are the high-end quadriplegics who don't have use of their arms. They control electric wheelchairs with their mouths. A small plastic tube is taken like a straw into the mouth, and they sip and puff. Like Morse code, variations of sucking and blowing into the tube command their chairs to move. I wonder what a sneeze would do.

My first electric chair was in the vanguard of a design revolution. Not only did it roll around, it could also magically transform into a La-Z-Boy recliner! The joystick controlled speed and direction, but also elevated the footrests and lowered the backrest. In that position I could take a nap, drain fluid from my ankles, which would get big and fat from edema, and take the pressure off my bottom. Sitting bolt upright in my chair would put a lot of pressure on my derrière. Skin needs blood to stay healthy, and lying back in the reclining position every half hour prevented the dreaded skin breakdown.

I was in mobile heaven! For all my pleadings as a kid, I never got a minibike or go-cart. Maybe I was reverting to my childhood with the thrill of this wheelchair. I would go out to the driveway and roll around just for the pleasure of feeling the wind at my face and centrifugal force pulling at me. I would do figure eights, circles, the daring high-speed dash, and the simple orbit.

This last maneuver was my favorite. I'd set the chair to spin in place automatically. Like a child twirling in circles until it falls down giggling in the grass, I would hold the joystick at hard right, spinning the chair in a tight circle with my eyes closed. Minutes would go by in a world that seemed timeless, until I got too dizzy to hold the joystick. I would always giggle and with a smile return to my ordinary life sitting on the throne of my magical wheelchair.

LET THE GAMES BEGIN

Time flies. Eight years later... my electric wheelchair was falling apart! The time had come for a new one; maybe an SUV wheelchair?

The vehicle I wanted to drive got twenty-five miles to a charge, but alas had only two-wheel propulsion. One brand actually came with tracks instead of wheels, like a tank. Unfortunately, it would've chewed up the carpet.

A power chair was such an important part of my life that I started the year and a half long process of justifying a $25,000 chair to Medicaid. Actually, my desired chair was nothing like a fancy SUV. It just had the basic, core features needed for me to be able to spend twelve hours a day in it.

In addition to an assessment from a physical therapist, I got letters from doctors, nurses, other medical professionals, and social workers, all supporting my cause. The physical therapist photographed me in the old chair to illustrate the reasons why I needed a new one. The local medical supply person wrote a twelve-page letter to Medicaid detailing my needs. Since requests for medical supplies were routinely denied, the supply company even hired a consultant who'd previously worked for Medicaid—turning down people's requests.

My request sailed through. Good thing, because I still owed money on my wheelchair van. I could never have afforded any kind of co-payment for a wheelchair, and I deeply needed a new one. In fact, the manufacturer had already stopped making the parts that would've allowed me to continue duct taping my old one together.

The new wheelchair was a Holy Grail for me. The old one just didn't fit me! I was hoping an appropriately fitting chair could relieve some of my severe back, hip and leg pain, and reduce skin breakdown. Because of my physical requirements, the chair I needed was top-of-the-line. I had to be able to lie flat, lift just my feet, tip back as in a regular chair leaned up against the wall, and roll faster than anyone could walk.

After meticulous body measurements, this was sure to be the first power chair that would fit my tall, lean frame. I knew it was going to be really comfortable. It had to be, in order for me to spend up to twelve hours a day in it.

After all my campaigning, I became the proud owner of my very own SUV, which got twenty miles to a charge (too bad it didn't come with leather seating, GPS, a massage feature, television, and four-wheel-drive). At long last, the Holy Grill was mine!

Like my new van, I knew Mr. Chair would be my last one, because like time, medical advances march on.

17

FOND MEMORIES OF THE FUTURE

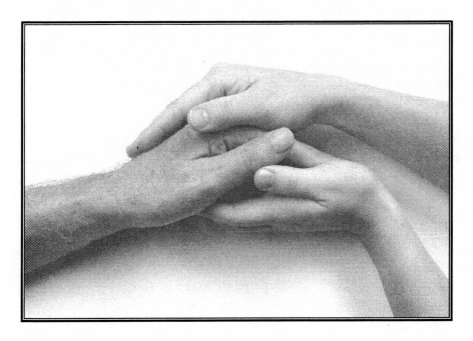

A book always needs a final chapter. How about a fictional finale? What could I see as the best of all circumstances? Well, I imagined the very best for myself and wrote it down.

As an ideal ending to this book, my fictional account envisions every aspect of a fulfilled life—love, health, and financial success through a creative livelihood. Using current medical wisdom from the experts, I hypothesized a cure for spinal cord injury from all that I've read and heard about advances in research.

This final chapter is about my future personal experience of learning how to walk again, and most of all, for the first time in my life, to love.

This story is set sometime within the first decade of the twenty-first century. Remember; this chapter is plausible fiction.

Rough Landing

The weather was turbulent around Cincinnati. I was flying coach, strapped bolt upright in my seat with three sturdy belts. An earache made itself known on the descent. Every thousand feet my head exploded with pain. Other body pains—from being immobilized for the nine-hour flight from Hawaii—clamored for my attention. But I could turn them all off with one thought: the cure.

Well, hopefully. Officially, I was going for beta testing of a promising treatment for spinal cord injury. A joint project between the University of Ohio at Cincinnati and a private research group had produced stunning successes with their first human trials three months prior. With 250,000 spinal cord injured in the U.S. alone, the research team kept a low profile to prevent being overrun with volunteers. I was able to slip in because of a "heads up" from a friend. He'd come across a few investment offerings from an associated biomedical company and suggested I contact the research project as a volunteer for treatment. I got on their list early (and bought some of the biomedical company's stock for good luck).

Early enough, that is, to say "no" to being an alpha research subject. Alpha people (going first) took the most risk. Beta people got the benefit of having some of the kinks already worked out of the system. I was too impatient to be a charlie or delta. Above all, I loved being with an Eve.

Stars in Her Eyes

Eve was preparing to give a lecture on trauma when she found my web site. She complimented my writing with an articulate, thoughtful e-mail. I responded in kind, and she responded back. This began a ping pong, back and forth communication by e-mail and telephone that had gone on for three years. For two of those years, little video cameras on our computers had given us moving pictures of each other. Our correspondence had grown to a profound depth and was to be fleshed out with a rendezvous in Cincinnati. Eve would be my training partner throughout the three months of clinical trials. She was joining me from Oxford, England, where she lived and worked as an American expat.

Eve met me at the Cincinnati airport. We already shared an alchemical connection from our lengthy correspondence, but once we were face to face at the airport, an even more enchanted dynamic took hold of us and began to simmer.

During one of our earliest moments alone, my soft gaze upon Eve's face snapped into a clear focus of her eyes. "Can I take you to lunch?" I grinned coyly, the blood draining from my face. With my next breath, a dragon climbed up my legs, through my belly and chest, and swirled inside my head. If she hadn't said "yes!" I'm sure this spiral of recognition would have condensed as tears in my eyes. I was sure my face had turned beet red. She was looking into my eyes and saying to my soul, "Let's play."

Eve was 5'3" and beautiful, with a radiantly feminine, round face, large, dramatic brown eyes graced with long eyelashes, and long, wavy black hair. Her petite frame was conditioned by a passion for running marathons. Even though we were eye level to each other, her heart and wisdom towered over me. She had degrees in comparative religion and psychology. During our time at the clinic, she would flesh out a research project entitled "Major Medical Crises: Direct Access to the Soul."

We were both smitten. I didn't know what to be more excited about, our late night snuggling or the fire spreading across my body from the injected cocktails.

A GROWING CONCERN

Following orientation, x-rays, and physical and psychological check-ups, Eve and I had settled into a routine of physical therapy and injections. People in white coats nodded in agreement at the success of our first phase of treatment. The daily injections of a cocktail, affectionately termed Kick-a-Poo Joy Juice by the eighteen people in our group, were working! This cocktail brew consisted of bioengineered stem cells and Schwann cells, plus three nerve growth stimulants. Some clever researchers found out that the secret for nerve growth in spinal tissue was to turn *off* the gene in the nerve cells that told the nerves *not* to grow. This reverse psychology was causing the injury to my spinal cord to disappear, as both sides were being chemically coaxed to grow through the implanted cells in search of fulfilling contacts on the other side. How romantic!

Initial growth of the nerve endings generated a fire throughout my body, very similar to the awakenings of an arm or leg that have fallen asleep, except that it was stronger and wouldn't go away. I felt like I had hives all over my body. A certain drug quieted the fire enough to be barely bearable by a bare-bottomed bear, but not for me. I was in pain!

Another drug was called out to tone down increasing body spasms and twitchings. For a while we looked like a clinic treating advanced Parkinson's disease. For more than a while, I needed heavy sedation just to sleep at night. I kept waking up thinking that somebody was jumping on my bed, only to see that it was my legs flopping about.

Even with Eve's encouragement, I began to doubt that I could continue keeping my sanity while the firestorm of nerves reconnecting raged on. She coined the phrase "The Fires of Rebirth," which became our mantra. If I wanted to walk again, could I go inside deep enough to find what it takes to survive the heat of being a chrysalis, and come out a butterfly?

Except for sleep, I was on fire twenty-four hours a day. I lost the use of my electric wheelchair, because my arms jerked uncontrollably like a newborn baby's and I couldn't control the joystick. I switched over to a manual chair, which was much slower and difficult to maneuver.

Wheelers from the alpha trial visited us for support. Most of their pain had subsided and they were in varying degrees of body control. It was a great relief every time an alphateer came into the room. They were like angels calling down from above, telling us we were on the right track and encouraging us to stay the course.

EMBRACING THE TIGER

"Try it again," cooed Eve, bracing my foot in her lap. I concentrated on the big toe. I was trying to consciously move it and had yet to succeed. General static kept my leg and foot squirming, but nothing moved due to my willful intention. I was in the newborn phase, according to the clinic's researchers. The spinal tissues were being encouraged to grow across the divide and connect with other nerves trying to meet halfway.

Unlike England and France's Chunnel connection, my nerves were connecting haphazardly. The fire came first as the nerves made contact, then the spasms followed as the nerves came to understand who was receiving and who was transmitting. Then the transmitting nerves had to get re-wired in the brain.

This was similar to a newborn baby's nervous system, sans fire. Their nerves are intact, but they still need to learn how to consciously control their bodies. Practice makes perfect for them—and for us.

The theory went that if you manually moved the limb, consciously pretending that the movement was of your volition, then the neural network agreed and hardwired the connection. We just didn't know when that would occur with the people in our trial. We were all unique, with different levels of injury and lengths of time injured.

"Eve, I've got to stop," I said, just shy of tears. "The pain is so great I can't concentrate. It's everywhere, and always seems greatest at the part I'm trying to move." We called over the clinician on duty. I wanted a pep talk.

"One of the keys to pain management is to go towards the pain and embrace it," said the white-coated person. "This sounds funny, but familiarity takes the edge off intense pain. If you can embrace it, Michael, as a friend who's helping you to walk, your pain will ease up." I knew he would say that, but I still felt better hearing it.

Another tool for pain management—distraction. Eve and I decided to stop early that day and go to a movie at the giziliaplex theaters down by the river. Cincinnati had long since renovated its riverside downtown area, where our medical center was located. We were just a short roll from the theaters and took the winding sidewalks along the river.

Eve rode on my lap, controlled the electric wheelchair, and cuddled us both up in a blanket to protect us from the cool fall weather. Her head leaned back to nuzzle my neck and I whispered into her ear, "I don't want to leave you. You're the most interesting person I've ever known, and I want to go deeper with you."

I smiled with a warm glow in my heart. "I feel the same way about you," she whispered back. Screwing up my courage to face rejection I said, "I would love it if you could come back to Maui with me."

Well, talk about a conversation starter. We never did get to that movie. We did stop at a couple of sidewalk cafes, where we talked and talked and fantasized and laughed and talked and laughed.

THIS LITTLE PIGGY...

The next day, Eve and I started yet another round of injections and took a tour of the assisted physical therapy equipment. I was strapped into various machines designed to mimic normal body movement. I went along for the ride and convinced myself that I was moving my legs. The continual practice of the mimicking movements slowly forged new neural connections to the brain. The more we worked with an area, the more connections were made, and slowly, thankfully, the fires cooled. Once the fires had retreated, our therapy went to twelve hours a day. It was harvest time—the more we invested, the more we got in return. This was getting fun.

After lunch we settled into the workout room. Beams of sunshine were streaming through one of the tall windows onto our station. Eve sat facing me and lifted my foot into position on her lap. I went into my routine of "moving" each toe, as she assisted.

Three minutes later we were both drop-jawed when my toe lifted, completely on my command, without Eve's help. We hugged and cried in each other's arms. The therapy was working! Everything was working! After years of relying upon blind trust to move me forward, we had the first tangible evidence that I would walk again.

I was awash with tears as Eve stood up in the middle of our group therapy room and yelled the required "Bingo!" at the top of her lungs. Everyone gasped and came over to see the proof of my toe moving the required three times. The cascading return had begun.

CHIPS AHOY

Everyone in our trial had new aches and pains; we'd been sitting down for so long. But lower body muscle strength and mobility were returning and with that, we faced a new challenge. Fragile bone mass was always in danger of breaking with the slightest infraction. Many in the trial had lost so much bone density that a casual fall could easily chip a hipbone. Any aged person will lose bone mass if they're not bearing weight on their bones. Astronauts returning from even short missions in space have noticeable bone loss.

We were given walkers, the fear of God about falling, calcium-boosting medications, and muscle strengthening exercises. The doctors counseled us to start very slowly back at home. Desperately weak muscles needed time to gain strength before being trusted to carry the body without assistance.

The good news was that pharmaceutical companies were bound for glory to help the baby boom generation handle arthritic pain and to reinforce the bones of the elderly with anti-osteoporosis drugs. Years of research had produced drug therapies that were stunningly successful in totally restoring lost bone density.

GOING HOME

At the end of three months we were asked to leave. The beta testers of the trial were to be replaced with the charlie company. No one felt completely healed, but at least the process had begun. We were given complete home therapy plans, along with an "800" number to a clinician. We were also invited back for check-ups every four months. No one knew how long this regeneration process would take.

We were cautioned at our final daily lecture not to expect a 100 percent, immediate return. "Celebrate the little successes that happen every day," declared the head of the program. "If your finger movement returns to grasping, celebrate all the different things you can lift. Walking should be the last thing to celebrate." I agreed. Walking was not as near a reality for me as using my fingers. Then I would be closer to the goal of becoming a paraplegic, after ten years of quadriplegia. (Isn't it a fun paradox to be sane and have paraplegia as an intermediate goal?)

On our last night at the clinic, after the final nursing check, Eve slipped into my room and cuddled up beside me. Her lips tickled my ear as she whispered a playful threat, "You cannot get rid of me, Mr. Kanouff"—as if I wanted to.

I interrupted, "I don't want to. Come to Maui. Play life with me." To have Eve as a life partner went beyond what I dared not want, for fear of angering the gods. "I'm honored to have you in my life," I said through a smile. After three years of correspondence and three months of intense, daily interaction, our love had grown to be bigger than the two of us. We both held the deep certainty that we'd found our true love. "I can't see a life where you're not walking by my side," I whispered to her. "Please stay with me, Eve."

"We'll never be parted," she whispered back. "You are the culmination, the crux intention, of my life's journey. I love you, Michael. And that will forever hold true."

Quadriplegics often get married and live full lives. But when you're a single quadriplegic and you're in bed alone at night, trying to slay the dragons of pain and fear, the belief that another person would want to join your life is hard to grasp. When the most beautiful goddess steps up and says that she wants to join that same life and merge with you in love, you'll never doubt the existence of a Higher Power again.

Reveling in the grace of it all, I held Eve and silently remembered how she'd moved elegantly and with good humor around all the people and processes of our life at the clinic.

One time, at the end of the day, she waited in the hallway until the doctor had completed some muscle testing with me, and then I whistled softly. Eve appeared at the door and I motioned her in with a flirtatious smile. "Hey you," she said like Lauren Bacall, pouncing and drawing my collar to meet her nose to nose. "Do we have time for a quickie before the guard gets back?" she purred.

"You bet, ninety seconds minimum," I said, looking left and right.

The ninety-second kiss slipped out of time because our eyes remained open, sending and receiving awareness with our breaths. When the door handle to our room turned, we giggled like kids and flaunted our attraction for each other to our friend the evening orderly.

I loved the way Eve brought out the best in me. She reached in and pulled me out of myself. In the past, slipping into rhythmic routines had seemed to be enough interaction with life, but really the routines lulled me to sleep, a waking sleep filled with deep pits of mediocrity. But I was excited to work on projects with her. Anything would do to keep our dance alive. At last, we had alchemically bonded to the one love of our lives, promised to us since birth. We both committed to being lifelong beloveds, having a personal relationship filled with the depths, not the limits, of spinal cord injury.

She wanted to continue her research work on Maui. There were about thirty spinal cord injured people to be part of her study concerning paralysis. As I pondered the possibilities of our new life, I was relieved we were going back to paradise for my recuperation. I began to wonder if others would come to Maui for therapy and recuperation.

MAUI ON MY MIND

Offshoots of this same clinical technology already had trials underway around the world, attacking the great scourges of dementia, Alzheimer's, stroke, MS, Spina Bifida, and the effects of alcoholism on the brain. We were entering the golden age of healthcare. Major medical breakthroughs brought on by rigorous stem cell research, the Genome Project, and subsequent gene therapy had revolutionized medicine. I was one of the pioneers who would remember spinal cord injury personally and talk about the "old days" before nerve regeneration therapy.

The time had come to clone the original clinic. If the upcoming charlie trials were successful, the process was close to being mass produced for the benefit of the quarter of a million spinal cord injured in the U.S. Eve and I had spoken with the heads of the clinic and we all felt the island of Maui to be a perfect location for one of the many satellite clinics. The process of healing there would be so clean and simple that Medicare, Medicaid, and insurance companies would jump to fund the three-month process in order to avoid the massive cost of long-term care for the spinal cord injured. What better place to go through a three-month therapy process than Maui?

Eve and I would be on the board as consultants and on the payroll as counselors at the beachside clinic where a client's first steps could be in the ocean. Also, a spectrum of repressed emotional issues might arise during a client's healing process that could be addressed during their stay at the clinic. Eve and I would help guide the client and their loved ones out of any unresolved emotional trauma in their lives. These issues percolate up to the surface of an individual and a family system when a life-threatening injury strikes.

ENVISION A BEAUTIFUL DAY

This chapter of fictional possibilities is a small segment of the vision I have for our future. I'm not living in denial of the present, just making sure I'm ready for the golden ring on the merry-go-round. I suggest this for anyone facing a medical crisis (or anyone for that matter). First, deeply appreciate what you already have by living each day fully. When there's time and energy, look forward and imagine your future with all its possibilities. This will be a defense to downward cycles of cynical thinking and give you momentum to look forward to life's gifts in whatever form they may come.

Again, it's anyone's guess as to the specifics of the cure for spinal cord injury. My heartfelt desire is that the therapy not require surgery with extensive teams of medical specialists; then only the wealthy and the newly injured would be cured for years to come.

A cure for spinal cord injury will be coming within another seven years. It could've been as soon as three years if religious conservatives hadn't pressured the junior Bush administration to choke off federal funding for stem cell research (and that's not just my humble opinion!). Thankfully, compassionate stem cell research continues moving forward in our country's private sector and in other civilized nations, most notably Israel. Hats off to England. Seeing the value of this type of research, the English government set up a state-sponsored bank for stem cell lines. But do keep in mind—they have security cameras everywhere.

The religious right's derailment of the United States government's research process for such a medically promising mode of treatment as stem cells is untenable. Even Nancy Reagan agrees that the delay would add years of suffering and cost many lives of those suffering from diabetes, Alzheimer's, MS, Lou Gehrig's disease, stroke, Spina Bifida, cancer and heart disease, to name just a few.

Stem cells can be grown not only from the leftovers of a fertility clinic, but also from adult skin cells and bone marrow cells. Some say that this is refining a technology that could eventually be used to clone humans. Well, let's cross that bridge when we come to it. Right now the world is suffering unnecessary pain and misery from diseases that are within our reach to wipe off the planet.

We have the technology to go forth but do we have the Will? Don't we all have a relative or friend suffering? Let's stop playing politics with millions of people's lives. Stem cells are the Silver Bullet. (If I just made you mad, I'm sorry. Try walking a mile in a wheelchair or living with a husband with Alzheimer's.)

If we had the national Will that developed projects Manhattan and *Apollo*, that same Will could pour research money into universities, medical facilities, and research corporations. Pure research blossoms into practical therapies that could personally touch every one of us. In the long run, the federal government would actually save money. Where is our vision? What do we value? What is important enough to spend our money and intellectual wealth on as a nation?

As we wait for the cure, I would like to see more care. Too many disabled people are warehoused and forced to live in an existential nightmare. The debate goes that if we give more care, less money goes to research. I'm not convinced this is so. Let's envision funds for both, until the day comes when we can all walk again and paralysis will fade from our memory like polio and smallpox.

In this brave new world, no one would have to be left in a state of disrepair, warehoused and out of sight. The overall physical health of our society would then leave us no excuse to avoid healing the real injury to us all—the wounding of our inner spirits, our souls.

Breakthroughs once inconceivable would light the hearts and souls of the emotionally damaged. An emotionally damaged soul is a time machine of unnecessary pain and suffering that is handed down through subsequent generations—an illness far worse than a spinal cord injury, which only lasts one generation.

The researchers who would refine these therapies and protocols were already walking the planet, and would go down in history as the midwives of the first generations of humanity who learned to shed their disabilities of pain and fear, to love to their highest potential. After that, walking would be a breeze.

CODA

*n. Music. A passage at the end of a movement
or composition that brings it to a formal close.*

I've heard from a consensus of wheelers (and have my own
experience), that it takes between five to seven years after a spinal
cord injury to come into a place of harmony and balance.
Physically, you've figured out how to manage your body, politically,
you're getting the most you can from your insurance company or social
service agencies, and emotionally, you've appreciated your new life.
Life can now be called "normal" and new branches can begin to grow
from your injured trunk. This new growth can be fresh and vital,
exceeding what you'd ever experienced before.

The Phoenix can rise from the ashes with features more grand and
glorious than known before. People are incredibly resilient and usually
strive to make the best of any situation. Maybe it's imprinted in our
genes, this impulse to do more, be better, raise our standard of living,
and help others in need.

In any case, pain and loss can temper the blade of one's inner mettle. This definitely applies to anyone undergoing the fires of paralysis. The majority of people who've suffered a major medical crisis have known intense pain. Most have put it in perspective and even used it to shape and improve their character. They can look through the fire to see that this momentous event can be the fast track to personal completion. Their new lives can be filled with profound meaning and purpose they'd never imagined before. These are some of the new limbs growing on a person in a wheelchair.

My most important branch to grow was that I fell in love—a true and lasting love. You never know when something good is going to happen to you. If you're paralyzed, I believe you are especially in line for grace and good fortune. Five years into my life as a quadriplegic, an American woman wrote me an e-mail letter from England, where she was living. In preparing for a series of lectures she was giving, she had read some of my earlier writing on paralysis via the Internet and wrote to compliment and congratulate me. It was such a knowing, perceptive letter I had to respond, and she responded back (Remember Eve? Well, truth inspired fiction.)

From our very first e-mails, we were both smitten. Countless more e-mails, telephone calls, photographs, and web cam conferences were to follow. After a year and a half of daily communication, she accepted my offer to visit me. Another extended visit followed six months later. Seven months after that, she closed her commitments overseas and moved to Maui. We remain deeply and profoundly in love. Even before my injury I was having doubts that I would truly find love in this lifetime. Throw becoming a quadriplegic into the mix and I thought having a beloved was impossible.

I keep pinching myself that such a beautiful, elegant, and educated woman as she could see my paralysis illuminated by my core personality. "Of course! Why not?" she exclaims. "Michael, I've known magical places and people from all over the world. The gift of that magic is that it brought me to a threshold of inner knowing about what I love and desire. And I fell in love with and desire you! With you Michael, I know I have my life's best." she concluded. Pinch, pinch, pinch, pinch...

I fell in love with her long black hair, stunning eyes, sharp mind, natural state of happiness that touches everyone she meets, and her soul. I finally know what love songs are all about, and I promise not to make fun of them anymore. She touches me deeply—to my soul—in every area of life. Finally, I know what they mean by the term "Soulmate." Our relationship continues to deepen day by day, with no end. There is a God and I know an angel!

Another branch of my new life that has grown lush with leaves is that I have a permanent house. It's large, comfortable, and in good condition. I'm proud to have this wonderful and accessible home. I also have a spacious and reliable van for transportation, and a computer to connect to the world. My studio has all the exercise equipment I need. My physical needs are covered.

Branches that were never injured and remain strong to this day are my extended family on Maui, my blood family in the Midwest, and of course living on this beautiful, tropical island of Maui.

The future looks brighter on the medical front. After ten years, I'm finally seeing a dramatic reduction of the pain in my body from sciatica, bladder infections, and ill-fitting wheelchairs. I'm relieved to see that branch withering.

I started writing these letters with the full intention of being completely honest about every aspect of life in the paralysis lane. What I've written is my truth. Something deeply personal, challenging, and rewarding has happened to me since my paralysis. After confronting the fact that I couldn't walk, my ego shattered into a million pieces. Only then, in the still silence, could I really hear myself and see the world in a different way. Maybe it wasn't really myself that I was listening to, but my Higher Self. I could put a face on it and call the experience listening to my deceased father, put another face on it and call it listening to God, or put another face on it and call it the Source.

The absolute best thing that can happen to anyone having a major medical crisis is that your normal world stops and your point of view changes. This new life gives you an opportunity to deepen your connection with loved ones, decide to let go of unhealthy relationships, or even, the Big Kahuna, release the pain that causes an addictive personality. It all depends on the individual, what one does with this surprise gift that wasn't brought by Santa.

I didn't wish to be paralyzed but I have to admit, I've grown tremendously through the experience of jumping quantum levels to the point that I can look around with confidence and know that I am now in the right place at the right time. The crucible of being spinal cord injured has been a trying one, and I am a better person for it. I've discovered that in the mysteries of love and life, everything is redeemed for good.

I hope you have enjoyed this reading. Except for the *#^%`*! editing, I have thoroughly enjoyed writing this book. Due to my injury, I discovered that I really enjoy expressing myself through the written word. Until the cure, my life will be experienced in a wheelchair. I will continue writing (and editing), adding chapters to my life's story. If you would like to continue reading, please contact me to be on the mailing list for my free, printed newsletter.

J. Michael Kanouff
Kanouff@Maui.net
or visit my web site
fromtheedge.net

APPENDIX A

CHRISTOPHER REEVE: SUPERMAN OR LEX LUTHOR?

Christopher Reeve acted in a commercial during the Super Bowl of 2000. He walked. I cried. His computer-animated body tottered across a stage to pick up an achievement award for his help in finding a cure for spinal cord injury sometime in the future. The commercial promoted investing in a medical research fund devoted to finding a cure for spinal cord injury. Charles Krauthammer, writing for *Time* magazine, expressed his problem with that, as summarized in the excerpt below. I follow with a rebuttal.

RESTORATION, REALITY, CHRISTOPHER REEVE
Dr. Charles Krauthammer

I have long been reluctant to criticize Christopher Reeve. I am not particularly keen to violate the Brotherhood of the Extremely Unlucky. (I injured my spinal cord when I was twenty-two.) But his Super Bowl ad was just too much.

For twenty-eight years I've been hearing that a cure is just a few years away. Being a doctor, I have discounted such nonsense. Yes, there is research... occasionally, there are some positive results in animal models. But the research is preliminary.

Yes, this research will bear fruit one day. The principal beneficiaries will be the newly injured. People long injured... will be the last to be helped. The cure will probably end up like the polio vaccine: preventing paralysis, not abolishing it. Even in the unlikely event there is a cure for those presently paralyzed, it will at best be partial. The idea so dramatized in the Super Bowl commercial that someone with a completely severed cord will actually walk is very far-fetched. Perhaps... some movement in the hands or chest or even legs. But it is far from the fantasy Reeve promotes: walking.

Reeve believes restoration is just around the corner. If he needs that to get through his day, who am I to disabuse him of his fantasies? But Reeve insists on parading his fantasies in public with the express purpose of converting others to them. In his public pronouncements and now in his disgracefully misleading Super Bowl ad, he is evangelizing imminent redemption.

Odder still if Reeve believes that people in wheelchairs don't dream enough about getting out of them. The newly paralyzed young might end up emulating Reeve, spending hours on end preparing their bodies to be ready to walk the day the miracle cure comes.

These kids should instead be spending those hours reading, studying and preparing themselves for the opportunities in the new world that high technology has for the first time in history made possible for the disabled.

They can have jobs and lives and careers. But they'll need to work very hard at it. And they'll need to start with precisely the psychological acceptance of reality that Reeve is so determined to undermine.

If I am wrong, the worst that can happen is that when the miracle comes, the nonbelievers will find themselves over trained and over toughened. But if Reeve is wrong, what will his dreamers be left with?

—from *Time* magazine, February 14, 2000

INVESTING IN A VISION
J. Michael Kanouff

It used to bother me. Minding my own business at public gatherings, I would endlessly be asked to sign some petition to end world hunger. I'd refuse, sensing a gimmick. If it was a project by a special interest group, well, all the more reason to be suspicious.

"No gimmicks, sir. Your signature acknowledges the possibility of ending world hunger in your lifetime," said the skinny young man in the white, short-sleeved shirt.

With a lifeless grin, my head shook no and I thought, "What's the good of just collecting signatures?"

I was living the early 80s in San Francisco and had a friend who worked with the inner circles of the EST organization, sponsors of the Hunger Project. After a mutual encounter with a petitioner to end world hunger, she told the story behind the endeavor.

There wasn't any specific fundraising to end world hunger; that would be too huge a project. What could be done with limited resources was to plant the idea in peoples' minds that it was possible—only that. To make a reality happen physically, the world needed first to have a vision, to have the seemingly impossible made real in our minds. The rest would follow.

I signed that petition and was ever after aware of news items dealing with third world economics and hunger. One night on television, I heard a stumping politician promising to end childhood poverty and hunger within ten years. "Hooray!" I yelled out to my housemates. The rich country would do it first. I rattled on about how the earth produced more than enough to end poverty and hunger. We had the means to feed everyone on the planet; it was the will and vision we were missing. Again, the effect of signing that petition rippled through twenty years of time with its continuing impact on me.

Another example of a vision in action: I was completely amazed on a bus one day when I read in the paper that President Carter's "Seed Bank" program had single-handedly turned a desperately poor, food importing country in Africa into a food exporting country within a few years' time! (Carter is very under appreciated.) By gathering up Western capital, he loaned individual landowners appropriate seeds, fertilizers and plows, and had them trained in specific irrigation and mulching techniques.

This was not a handout, but a loan. The first year families fed themselves. Their excess crop on the second year bought more equipment, seeds, and fertilizer. After the third year, they paid back their loans. In a few years more, the country was growing enough to earn money exporting its surplus crop. Now who was the real hero?

Carter used his organizing skills to begin this grassroots momentum of change, but who whispered the idea into his ear? Who had Carter's full attention long enough to describe a vision real enough for him to act upon? (Probably Rosalynn, but that's another story.)

My home, the island of Maui, was having a boom cycle in real estate during the 90s. Incredibly wealthy Japanese investors were buying up anything that didn't run away. Then their economy faltered, and property prices plummeted.

But another real estate up cycle was soon to follow. The newer buyers also spoke an exotic tongue—that of .com, .net, and other basic vocabulary of binary language. High tech mainland America was getting so wealthy, Maui was being flooded by baby boomers buying their second and third houses for investment!

Where to invest became the party conversation topic of Maui residents because of the trickle down wealth. From realtors to massage therapists, people on Maui suddenly had extra income. They also had the nagging worry of not having anything set aside for retirement. Huge segments of the Maui baby boomers, once used to living hand to mouth, were flush with this newly earned, quick money, and were eagerly asking each other, "Where are you investing?" (In their innocence, some were even investing in offshore banks that offered 80 to 120 percent return—every year! Yeah, right. And I had a bridge for sale.)

Across the country, this explosion of wealth had to be spent, saved, or invested. Eventually, their research would convince investors what area of the world economy to support with the new excess money in their lives. A few hundred thousand of them probably had a common idea form during a twenty-first century tournament of gladiators. Their full attention was glued to yet another stunning Super Bowl commercial. Thirty seconds of swirling images, sounds, and emotion probably changed the life direction of thousands of people by implanting an idea: invest in medical research funds and companies!

The Christopher Reeve commercial burned an enduring image of him walking again into our collective psyche. In one fell swoop, hundreds of thousands of people knew that there was another industry worth the investment of their money. In addition to financially supporting companies producing razor blades, petroleum, and electronic everything, they could invest in the field of biomedical research. Also, investment in biomedical research companies supports the health of humanity and doesn't strip-mine the raw material wealth of the planet.

Dr. Krauthammer, fearing the harm this vision would have on the newly injured young wrote, "(They) might end up... spending hours on end preparing their bodies to be ready to walk the day the miracle cure comes."

The newly injured young have to believe in walking again. Vision above and beyond present circumstance is the survival skill of any healthy personality thrust into the unknown. Belief in the cure and a higher vision of good keeps them facing away from the black hole of horrific, mind-numbing darkness, where they're told to skirt along the edge for the rest of their lives, and toward the living. Their positive attitude of hopeful expectation overflows into the lives of their loved ones and continues to ripple out into the rest of society.

The newly injured young will make any effort and try any experimental therapy to keep their bodies in shape. The hope of an imminent cure is the life preserver that holds their heads above the dark waters of despair. This "protective denial" and its feverish attempts usually last for one to two years, before boredom sets in.

Then they are naturally drawn to what Dr. Krauthammer calls "... preparing themselves for the opportunities in the new world that high technology has for the first time in history made possible for the disabled." Those that do spend their first years rigorously preparing for the cure, like Mr. Reeve, tend to maintain their physical fitness while retooling to live in our brave, new, high technology world. By the way, these high technology interfaces for the disabled exist only because someone once had a vision and drew investors to their side.

Both Christopher and his wife Dana were briefed on the advances of leading edge medical technologies. They knew the inestimable value of investment capital flowing into groundbreaking research organizations at a critical time. With glaring genius, the Reeves used this commercial of Christopher walking to insert a vision into our society. They couldn't raise all the money by themselves, but they could plant a vision of what's possible in our lifetime.

Mr. Reeve was shown rising above the ashes of one of humanity's most trying fires. He made many of us become believers in the miraculous image of the broken walking again.

Even if Dr. Krauthammer doesn't believe in a cure, why disparage anyone's efforts to draw financial capital into the biomedical field, which will literally help millions of people in the future?

The technology and the will to overcome medical hurdles are unstoppable. Raising capital for research, development, treatment and cure requires investors with a vision of humanity rising above the ashes of paralysis, Parkinson's, Alzheimer's, stroke, MS, cancer, heart disease, and so many other conditions. This can be done in our lifetime.

"Would you sign here, please?" said the thin investment counselor wearing a white shirt.

"It is time that we create positive images about the miracles that scientific research can bring. Negativism or dashing hopes never cured a disease. My hope is that people will be energized by the power of the story in this commercial. It is a vision of what can actually happen."

Christopher Reeve

APPENDIX B

RESOURCES

Rather than trying to make a definitive list of resources, this section describes my approach to culling information. These are principles distilled from my own experience that might be pertinent to others gathering data and getting perspective.

When a physical health problem erupts in a family, they develop an insatiable hunger for knowledge. The short audience with the doctor is never enough. They want more. No one has to go it alone and reinvent the wheel. This is the era to appreciate the "interdependence" of humanity, rather than the independent isolation of the individual.

Make friends with other wheelers in town for valuable local information. They'll have experience about support groups, physicians familiar with spinal cord injuries, good places to buy medical supplies, and how to make the best of the local social services.

Of all the eras in human history, I picked a pretty terrific time to get injured. My new life as a quadriplegic began at about the same time the Internet was just beginning to take hold. It has since matured to become the single most valuable resource for outside information. Each individual forms their own relationship to the flood of information on the web and will be drawn to particular sites. The Internet is very fluid and ever changing, so I can only recommend four specific sites that will not fade away into the sunset.

Christopher and Dana Reeve opened the Paralysis Resource Center (www.paralysis.org), which is basically a clearinghouse of information for people who need or want to learn about living with paralysis. So if, for example, somebody needs to find an accessible van rental company near where they live in Idaho, or if they need a doctor in Hoboken, an accessible condo on Maui, etc., they can call the Resource Center for help. This site will remain a constant source for state-of-the-art information about the practical side of dealing with spinal cord injury. Judging by the founders, this is a resource that you can bookmark and completely trust.

For information about cutting edge research and quality of life programs, investigate the Christopher Reeve Paralysis Foundation web site (www.christopherreeve.org). Both sites offer free newsletters.

173

The third site, which has a stable, ten-year track record is hosted by the organization called New Mobility (www.newmobility.com). In addition to a monthly magazine, this web site offers a wealth of information and hosts a vigorous discussion group. I like to eavesdrop to search for a specific topic and gather firsthand information.

The fourth Internet site that has quality information and staying power is Paralinks (www.paralinks.net). I'm proud to know Gary Schooley, the heart and soul of this electronic magazine. A paraplegic since 1979, Gary scours the Internet for listings of folks with spinal injuries telling their personal experiences—their stories of how they survived and thrived after this major event in their lives.

Start with these sites and then go on your own search. You will get information overload, plus a soothing balm that you're not alone. Bookmark useful information, and keep your bookmarks organized. You may come across something not needed at the moment, but that you may wish for later on.

In addition to the official government and private web sites dealing with every aspect of spinal cord injury, check out the unofficial sites, the paralysis discussion groups. Simply type "Spinal Cord Injury Discussion Groups" into any search engine, and explore a few. You can just eavesdrop for general information, or search for specific conversations on topics directly concerning you.

It's refreshing to hear others honestly speaking their own opinions about all topics related to spinal cord injury. You can even throw out your own question to hundreds of other wheelers for their input. But beware—discussion groups are also open to those who are angry and cynical. See these people for who they are and search on for positive input. Most wheelers are eager to help someone else save some time, money, or misery by sharing their relevant experience.

It's a brave new computerized world for all of society, but a word of caution to the recently paralyzed—don't be lulled into virtual excess and away from human contact. Keep your dreams and desires in front of you and take action steps, even baby steps, every day towards a goal. Your goals may change as time goes by, and that's OK. The important thing is that you keep moving forward and interacting with your loved ones, community, and the world around you.

Avoid snake oil salesmen and going to Mexico for miracle surgeries. Brazil is off limits too, for its shamanic trance healers. Also stay away from Philippino doctors who pull chicken guts out of people's necks and proclaim the departure of evil spirits. Keep your distance from fundamentalist healing ministries that pack auditoriums by using stagefuls of empty wheelchairs as props. They might put on a good TV spectacle, but can't actually regenerate spinal tissue.

If you choose not to keep up with advances in spinal cord research, that's OK too. Go about life becoming your best and help others who might be falling behind. When the cure comes, you'll know about it. It will be news around the world and Barbara Walters will be interviewing Christopher Reeve.

FURTHER READING

Beisser, Arnold R. *Flying Without Wings*. Bantam, 1990.

As an early pioneer into the world of quadriplegia, Arnold Beisser gives us a clear look at being paralyzed from both sides of the medical model. He graduated from medical school and became an early victim of polio. After surviving rehab hospitals, he went on to pursue a career in psychiatry.

The book describes Arnold's search to find a new life and new meaning for himself, without at first knowing how or where to begin. Taking us on his journey, he provides a useful guide for anyone faced with loss, pain, disability, and the imminence of death. He shows us that peace, humor and joy can appear at any moment. As a professional caregiver of the mind, his honest perspective of his own physical caregivers is especially poignant.

Bradshaw, John. *Homecoming*. Bantam, 1992.

A physical life crisis brings upon us the obvious trials particular to our illness. It also brings out our core psychological personalities. Fears and phobias can be accentuated and threaten fragile relationships with family, who are often thrust into the caregiving role.

The author describes with great clarity how to help reclaim, champion, and heal the wounded inner child within us. He details the developmental stages from birth through adulthood and illumines how we come to abandon who we are when confronted with a dysfunctional family setting.

Several questionnaires and exercises guide you to your destination. Instructions are given for working alone, with a partner, or with a group.

Dyer, Wayne. *Real Magic*. HarperTorch, 1993.
_____. *Your Sacred Self*. HarperTorch, 1995.
_____. *Manifest Your Destiny*. HarperTorch, 1997.
_____. *You'll See It When You Believe It*. Quill, 2001.
_____. *There's a Spiritual Solution to Every Problem*. Quill, 2002.
_____. *The Power of Intention*. Hay House, 2004.

These are some of the many books and tapes Dr. Wayne Dyer has created to inspire and lift the human spirit. Dr. Dyer, affectionately called the "father of motivation" by his fans, is one of the most widely known and respected people in the field of self-empowerment. Despite his childhood spent in orphanages and foster homes, Dr. Dyer, who has a doctorate in counseling psychotherapy, has overcome many obstacles to make his dreams come true.

A medical crisis will stop your everyday normal world and give you the opportunity to look deep inside yourself for meaning and relevance. When life gives us lemons we might as well sweeten our situation with inspirational books, tapes, music, and movies. Add to the mix supportive family and good friends, and your life crisis won't seem so ominous.

I speak from personal experience that Dr. Dyer's books and tapes helped me keep from spiraling into a pit of depression after my spinal cord injury. Any of his publications will speak to you if you're facing a medical crisis or just the daily commute. I am also honored to call him my friend.

Hockenberry, John. *Moving Violations*. Hyperion, 1996.

Journalist John Hockenberry's exceptional prose reflects a witty, intelligent, and perceptive spirit. He deftly takes on sex and challenges people's perceptions of and mental blocks toward the disabled. For example, many expect all those who are paralyzed to entertain suicidal thoughts. Hockenberry counters, "I never once contemplated suicide. Suicide is something you argue yourself out of, not into."

This stirring account of surmounting hearty obstacles—both physical and emotional—is a monument to human resilience.

Jampolsky, Gerald G. *Love Is Letting Go of Fear*. Celestial Arts, 1988.

A classic of gentle simplicity, this book can keep a newly injured person and their loved ones from tailspinning into depression. Based on material from *A Course in Miracles*, this book teaches us how to let go of fear and how to remember that our very essence is love. Included are daily exercises that give a direct and effective method for bringing about individual transformation.

Karp, Gary and Klein, Stanley D. *From There to Here*. No Limits
    Communications, 2004.

Forty-five people. Forty-five diverse yet personal life stories. All
of them are connected by a powerful, shared life experience—spinal
cord injury.

From There To Here is certainly about hope—but not by way of
mere inspiration. These essays are the stuff of whole human lives, and
illustrate the real and complex process of how people respond to
sudden and overwhelming change. They start from trauma and
confusion, their vision of the future challenged to the core, and
ultimately arrive at a place that each of them in their own way calls
"adjustment." A place that none of them could have imagined when
they were There. The heart of these stories is what happened in
between—the actual journey to adjustment, acceptance, meaning, and
possibility. The journey to Here.

Kübler-Ross, Elisabeth. *On Death and Dying*. Simon & Schuster, 1969.

A physical life crisis need not lead to death, but it does bring up
similar issues around our mortality. Ours is a death-denying society.
But death is inevitable. Even in a symbolic death, such as illness or
injury, we must face the question of how to deal with dying. Coming to
terms with our own finiteness helps us to discover life's true meaning.

Why do we treat death as a taboo? What is the source of our fears?
How do we express our grief, and how do we accept the death of a
loved one? How can we prepare for our own death?

Drawing from various cultural perspectives on death and dying,
Kübler-Ross provides some illuminating and thought-provoking
answers to these and other questions. She offers a spectrum of
viewpoints, including those of ministers, rabbis, doctors, nurses and
sociologists, along with personal accounts of those nearing death and
then their surviving loved ones.

Once we come to terms with our own life crises as being facets of
death that can break us free from the constricting aspects of a former
life, we can see dying as a crucial part of being alive. The author guides
us to the knowledge that death and dying can provide us with a key to
the meaning of human existence.

Levine, Peter A. *Waking the Tiger, Healing Trauma*. North Atlantic
    Books, 1997.

This book offers a new and hopeful vision of trauma. It views the
human animal as a wondrous being, endowed with amazing instinctual
capacities. Levine asks and answers a central intriguing question—why
are animals in the wild, though threatened routinely, rarely
traumatized? By understanding the dynamics that make wild animals
immune to traumatic symptoms, the mystery of human trauma is
revealed.

People often experience the toxic effects of cumulative trauma.
Waking the Tiger presents the symptoms of human trauma and the
steps needed for healing. The reader is taken on a guided tour of the
subtle yet powerful impulses that govern our responses to traumatic life
events. To do this, Levine employs a series of exercises that draws the
reader's focus to deep, bodily sensations. Through a heightened
awareness of these sensations and a release of their toxicity, trauma can
be healed.

Price, June. *AVOIDING Attendants from HELL*. Science & Humanities
    Press, 1998.

As accessible housing and supportive services become increasingly
available, people with physical disabilities have a growing opportunity
to move out of their parents' homes or institutions and live
independently. But true independence is dependent upon the degree and
quality of personal care assistance available. *AVOIDING Attendants
from HELL* is a comprehensive, "how to" hiring guide for individuals
who are physically disabled, as well as a valuable resource for
professional caregivers and supportive family members involved in the
independent living process.

Reeve, Christopher. *Still Me*. Ballantine Books, 1999.

Publishers Weekly has this to say:
"A memoir that's outspoken, wise, and tremendously
moving... Writing in a clean, even, matter-of-fact style that renders his

words all the more devastating for their lack of bathos, Reeve reveals the intimacy of his plight... No doubt Reeve is 'still me'—but readers of his beautifully composed book will see that he is now also more; that through nearly unimaginable suffering and effort, he has transformed a charmed life into one blessed to be a true profile in courage."

Reeve, Christopher. *Nothing Is Impossible*. Random House, 2002.

An Amazon.com commentary reads:

"Christopher Reeve has mastered the art of turning the impossible into the inevitable. In *Nothing Is Impossible*, the author of the best-selling autobiography *Still Me* shows that we are all capable of overcoming seemingly insurmountable hardships. He interweaves anecdotes from his own life with excerpts from speeches and interviews he's given and evocative photos taken by his son Matthew.

Reeve teaches us that for able-bodied people, paralysis is a choice—a choice to live with self-doubt and a fear of taking risks—and that it is not an acceptable one. Reeve knows from experience that the work of conquering inner space is hard and that it requires some suffering—after all, nothing worth having is easy to get. He asks challenging questions about why it seems so difficult—if not impossible—for us to work together as a society. He steers the reader gently, offering his reflections and guidance but not the pat answers that often characterize inspirational works."